How to
Rescue
The Earth
Without
Worshipping
Nature

HOW TO RESCUE THE EARTH WITHOUT WORSHIPPING NATURE

A Christian's Call to Save Creation

TONY CAMPOLO

WORD PUBLISHING

Word (UK) Ltd
Milton Keynes, England

WORD AUSTRALIA
Kilsyth, Victoria, Australia

STRUIK CHRISTIAN BOOKS (PTY) LTD
Maitland, South Africa

JOINT DISTRIBUTORS SINGAPORE –
ALBY COMMERCIAL ENTERPRISES PTE LTD
and
CAMPUS CRUSADE

CHRISTIAN MARKETING NEW ZEALAND LTD
Havelock North, New Zealand

JENSCO LTD
Hong Kong

SALVATION BOOK CENTRE
Malaysia

HOW TO RESCUE THE EARTH
WITHOUT WORSHIPPING NATURE

First published in the USA by Thomas Nelson, Inc., Nashville, Tennessee.

Word (UK) Ltd. edition 1992.

ISBN 0-85009-571-9 (Australia ISBN 1-86258-221-1)

All Scripture quotations are from the New King James Version of the Bible, Copyright © 1979, 1980, 1982, Thomas Nelson, Inc., Publishers.

Printed and bound in Great Britain for Word (UK) Ltd. by Cox & Wyman Ltd., Reading.

93 94 95 / 10 9 8 7 6 5 4 3 2

In honor of
John David Burton,
my friend and first mentor,
whose sermons and poetry bring
inspiration and insight into all
of God's creation

CONTENTS

vii

PREFACE

It took evangelical Christians a long time to wake up to the fact that the Bible calls us to be socially responsible. I hope and pray that it does not take as long to realize that the Bible also calls us to be environmentally responsible. Too much is at stake and the time is very short.

The reason for the absence of environmental concerns in both our beliefs and our actions is probably due to accepting a theology in which, to use J. B. Phillips's expression, "Our God is too small." We evangelicals have preached a God who sent His Son into the world to save us, but we have been reluctant to grasp the biblical truth that His salvation was meant for more than humans. Our sermons have taught that God loves people and wills to rescue them from sin and Satan, but in our homilies, we have ignored the message of God's saving work for the rest of His creation.

It is time for the world to know that when John 3:16 declares that "God so loved the world," the word *world* in this verse is, in the original biblical language, the word *cosmos*. The salvation that John 3:16 talks about is for everything in the universe, not just for people.

This book is not only about a Savior who came into the world to make us into people who can love and worship His Father; it is also about a Savior who came to deliver the rest of creation from its "groanings" so that it too can offer up worship to God.

This book is about a Jesus whose salvation has cosmic dimensions. It is about a call to Christians to participate with their Lord in making this salvation known.

Joining me in putting this book together was my good friend and editor, Lonnie Hull. My niece, Debra Davidson, did most of the typing; and my former assistant and good friend, Mary Noel Keough, together with Pat Carroll, Kristin Winch-Peterson, and Lisa Kjeldgaard, helped out with the final draft. My wife, Peggy, did the proofreading and first editing. Finally, there are the good people at Eastern College where I teach. Without the support of Eastern's President Roberta Hestenes and Provost Ward Gasque, I would never have had the freedom to put in the time that such a book requires. I am most grateful to all of these people.

As I wrote this book, I had the sense that I was charting some new territory or at least rediscovering some forgotten truths. I felt that I was not simply exploring some new dimensions of commonly accepted Christian doctrine but that I was venturing into whole new ways of thinking and picking up some biblical themes that had been laid aside for too long. There was, in fact, a kind of giddy excitement about all of this. My hope is that, as you read this book, you will pick up some of those same feelings.

TONY CAMPOLO
Eastern College
St. Davids, Pennsylvania
April 1992

GETTING INTO IT

Why This Book Is the Most Important I've Ever Written

What do you think is the most important issue that Christians will have to face in the next ten years?" I asked.

Four of us sat around a small table in a hoagie shop in West Philadelphia. We were taking a break from an all-day meeting of evangelical leaders who had gotten together to discuss the future of the church. The two men and one woman who had joined me for a snack were among the smartest and most effective leaders in Christendom, and I figured that this was my chance to learn their opinions on "hot" topics.

Without hesitation, Tom Sine, an outstanding author and futurologist, shot back, "The environment!"

The other two immediately agreed. This surprised me since one of those at the table was Ron Sider, author of *Rich Christians in an Age of Hunger*. I thought he would certainly have said something like hunger or poverty. But, no! He, too, said, "The environment." I must add that he then went on to explain that if the destruction of the environment continues, more and more arable land will not be available to grow food. Then only the rich would eat, and the number of starving poor people would increase by the millions.

Martha Lyon simply commented that the environment had become a primary concern of youth. "Paying attention to the environment," she commented, "is something that young people make us do."

But friends of mine are not the only ones who are telling me that the destruction of the environment is becoming the most important issue of our time. Paul Brand, the famous medical missionary who has spent his life treating lepers in India, says the same thing: "The world will die from lack of soil and pure water long before it will die from lack of antibiotics or surgical skill and knowledge."[1]

This is an amazing statement coming from someone who has seen the suffering of poor people in Third World countries where there are too few doctors and too little medicine. When this medical missionary, whose brilliant service for Christ has been chronicled in articles and books, makes a statement like this, it behooves all of us to sit up and take notice. And if *you* stop to think about it, you probably will agree with him.

You know what we're doing to this fragile little planet of ours. You read the papers. You know how we're destroying the land that gives us food, polluting the air that we breathe, and contaminating the rivers that give us our drinking water. I don't have to pound you with facts and figures. You know that the problems related to the destruction of the environment are now severe. And what is making matters worse is that people in general, and Christians in particular, don't seem to care. Even though Christians have been commissioned by God to be good stewards of His creation, they appear to be the least concerned with what is going on. And of all the Christians, those who call themselves evangelicals have the worst record. Studies show that the more zealously committed people become to evangelical churches, the less concerned they are about the horrible things that are happening to the environment. We "Bible-believing, born-again, Spirit-filled Christians," more than any others, seem to have turned deaf ears to the pleas to save God's creation from what has to be called sinful exploitation.

Denton Lotz, general secretary for the Baptist World Alliance, says, "There seems to be a conflict between those who emphasize saving souls and those who emphasize saving trees." He concludes, "This is a ridiculous conflict. We need saved souls who can live a meaningful life in God's beautiful world of nature which is yearning to be free from pollution."[2]

Lotz goes on to say, "Let's not confuse evangelism with ecology, but let's also show that true evangelists are also true ecologists."

WHAT SCARED ME ABOUT WRITING THIS BOOK

When I decided to write a book on the environment, I knew I was opening myself up to criticism. I realized that there were those who, at best, would label me as someone seduced by the New Age movement. At worst, my critics would condemn me as a demonic influence within the circles of evangelical Christianity. Since the New Age movement has made much of the ecological movement, some church folks are ready to claim that anybody who is concerned about the environment must be into New Age thinking. Anyone who happens to espouse a cause that is already on the agenda of a deviant religious movement, no matter how biblically based that cause might be, is often declared a heretic.

This stupidity is intolerable. Of course, those in the New Age movement are often deeply committed to the same environmental concerns which are the focus of this book. But only those with fuzzy minds would fail to see the error of condemning someone simply because he or she supports a good cause that enemies of the faith support. Only those who are devoid of logic would conclude that we must have nothing to do with anything embraced by those whose religion is questionable. Obviously, if we yield to these kinds of judgments, we would have to disengage from every good cause the minute our ideological and spiritual opponents identify with it.

On the other hand, I must be careful not to defensively overreact. There really *is* a tendency for many Christians, who become "green" in their activism and commit themselves to making environmental issues a vital part of their faith, to also become seriously confused in their thinking. I must be ready to admit that there really is some truth to the accusation that some green Christians end up talking very much like New Agers and in time end up espousing some New Age theology.

Since Christians who desire to carry out their biblically prescribed responsibilities for creation seldom have many partners in the church, they often end up doing most of their talking and thinking with those who are the exponents of the strange New Age ideas which seem more and more evident in our society. And often, because of lack of Christian literature on the subject, they turn to books about the environment published by New Age authors. Consequently, there are some red flags of warning for those Christians who want to take creation more seriously. As you read on, you will find that I wave these red flags vigorously.

I am worried that Christians who get involved in the environmental issue may get side-tracked into the "pop" religious thinking of the New Age movement. But I am also worried that Christians may turn their backs on what is quickly becoming the most crucial issue of our time. I am worried that our indifference to the destruction of God's creation will allow a bunch of New Age gurus to hijack a movement that should be ours.

We Christians can't let this one get away from us. We lost a lot of people because we responded to the civil rights movement too slowly. We lost even more because we said too little too late about the war in Vietnam. At this present time, we can't ignore something that will be a vital concern, not only to those whom critics mockingly label "eco-freaks," but also to huge masses of people in America and throughout the world.

A CHRISTIAN OBLIGATION

My main reason for writing this book is that I want to add my voice to an increasing chorus which declares that rescuing the environment from an impending disaster is biblically mandated and that ending the careless selfish life-style that has brought us to this impending

disaster is a Christian obligation. I want to help bridge
the gap that now exists between many evangelicals and
many environmentalists who often tend to view each
other with suspicion. I want to show that Christianity at
its best is environmentally responsible. By the time I fin-
ish, I hope you will so connect evangelical thinking with
"creation-care" that it will be impossible to be in the one
without being in the other.

In order to accomplish this task, I want you to join
me as together we sort through a host of ideas and beliefs that have come from sources as diverse as hard
empirical scientists and Christian mystics. This journey
will take us back in time to the thinking of St. Francis
and St. Benedict. We will explore the contributions to
the theology of creation made by some of the historic
founders of Protestantism, such as John Calvin and
John Wesley. We will also give attention to C. S. Lewis
and Pierre Teilhard de Chardin, who represent more
modern Christian thinking.

Our search for a Christian understanding of creation
and our responsibility for its care will take us into some
of the largely untapped beliefs of our brothers and sisters in the Eastern Orthodox churches. Indeed, our quest
will require that we be very ecumenical and cross those
barriers that have separated Protestants and Catholics,
pentecostals and evangelicals, as well as liberals and
fundamentalists. We will try to glean biblically based
truths wherever they may be found.

In all of this, I want to set this task of creation-care in
the context of Christian spirituality. I want you to come
away from reading this book with a sense that there is
no way that you can be faithful to Scripture and sensitive to the leading of the Holy Spirit without becoming
involved in the efforts to rescue the environment. I want

to make it clear that to evidence the "fruit of the Spirit" (Galatians 5:22–23), you must be a person who empathizes with the sufferings of all of God's creation and who makes praying for the deliverance of creation from its bondage to evil (Romans 8:21) a part of your devotional life. I hope you will be motivated to enter into a new kinship with nature and through this kinship, to worship God in new ways.

Finally, I will try to outline some appropriate Christian responses to the environmental crisis and give some limited suggestions of specific things that we can do to participate with God in saving planet earth. These suggestions will be things we can do in our churches, things we can do as individuals, and things we can do in the political arena. And in the end, I hope that together we will be able to understand the psalmist and join with him and the rest of creation in singing:

> Praise the LORD!
> Praise the LORD from the heavens;
> Praise Him in the heights!
> Praise Him, all His angels;
> Praise Him, all His hosts!
> Praise Him, sun and moon;
> Praise Him all you stars of light!
> Praise Him, you heavens of heavens,
> And you waters above the heavens!
> Let them praise the name of the LORD,
> For He commanded and they were created.

> (Psalm 148:1–5)

2

CHICKEN LITTLE WAS RIGHT

Facing an Environmental Disaster

The world is becoming dirty and ugly, and it's time to do something about it. The air is being turned into smog. The rivers are polluted. Toxic chemicals fill the soil. The oceans have become garbage dumps, and trash is piling up on the edges of our cities.

In America, more than seven million cars are junked every year. In New York alone, there are over seventy thousand abandoned cars on the streets. We throw away forty billion metal cans, twenty-six billion bottles, and sixty-five billion bottle caps annually. Indestructible plastic appears everywhere. Oil spills pollute our beaches, and chemical rain and expanding industry destroy our rain forests.

But these facts and figures do not seem to upset us at all until the dirtiness and ugliness invade our everyday lives.

Frank Rizzo, the politically conservative and extremely controversial mayor of Philadelphia, at one time tried to ignore those seeming prophets of doom who talked about the mess we were making of God's creation. "Big Frank," as we Philadelphians called him, had names like "weirdos" and "pinko crazies," along with less polite designations, for those who joined Greenpeace, the Sierra Club, or other "consciousness raising" organizations that were always making such a fuss over the environment. As far as Frank was concerned, the people who got agitated about such things were usually those "pointed-head, intellectual leftists" who were always making trouble for the rest of us. In some way he couldn't quite explain, these "eco-freaks" were "unpatriotic."

All of this changed for Philadelphia Mayor Frank Rizzo the day his dog got sick. He loved his dog and was beside himself when the animal was rushed to a veterinary hospital. Rizzo cried when his dog died. The veterinarian explained that chemicals in the lawn fertilizer had caused the dog's sickness and death. Then the mayor got *mad!* He called a press conference and said loud and clear, "I don't think those environmentalists are crazy anymore. I'm one of them!"

Sooner or later we will all get caught up in the environmental movement, because sooner or later we will all get hurt by what is happening to nature. I suppose that becoming a grandfather has heightened my concern about the destruction of the beauty and ecological balance of our planet. I wonder what kind of world will be waiting for my grandchildren when they come of age. Will I have to tell them about whales because there are none for them to see? Will there be no more mountain gorillas in Africa? Will the trees be devoid of singing birds?

In the midst of such speculations, I cannot help but ask myself, *What is so important for me to have that I am willing to sacrifice the future of my children and grandchildren in order to get it?* Do I so desire to maintain my affluent, wasteful life-style that I do not care if my heirs have to live in a cancer-causing, filthy environment? Am I so in love with the things that the media convinces me I want that I am indifferent to the devastation to the environment that results from their production?

In 1962, Rachel Carson published her now famous book, *Silent Spring*. In that book, she sounded an alarm that caught the attention of millions. For the first time, large numbers of people became aware of the fact that DDT and other chemicals used to fight insects and to treat the soil poisoned birds and other animals. Carson made it clear that unless we took some drastic steps to change things, entire species of birds and other animals which add beauty, music, and joy to our lives would become extinct.

Smog alerts are becoming increasingly common in cities across the country. Exhaust from automobiles and soot from industrial smokestacks render the air so putrid that it becomes dangerous to breathe. People with respiratory problems are warned to stay inside, preferably in air-conditioned rooms. There are frequent deaths that result from simply breathing the air on "bad" days. Anyone who regularly flies recognizes the unmistakable brown layer of smog hovering over such cities as Los Angeles and Denver.

Something has gone wrong with the weather. It is getting slightly warmer with each passing decade. What we are doing to the atmosphere has created a phenomenon we have dubbed the "greenhouse effect." Without going into a deep explanation at this point, the greenhouse effect is the net result of carbon dioxide from exhaust fumes that is increasing in the upper layers of the atmosphere.

Soda pop cans to styrofoam containers from McDonalds trash our once-beautiful beaches. The bacteria count in the water has become so great that beach closings are now common. Along the New Jersey shore, sewage, pharmaceutical containers, and other forms of medical waste dumped into the ocean wash up regularly on the sand.

A list of impending ecological disasters is readily available, yet there has been little response from the church. And, as I have already stated, studies indicate that Christian people are least likely to be concerned about the environment. Evangelical Christians seem to show the greatest indifference. In the face of this catastrophe, there are still Christians who think that being committed to saving God's creation is something that goes with being a bit offbeat. Worse than that, when some of us talk about saving the planet earth, some church people whisper under their breath, "I think our friends are slipping away from true Christianity."

Contemporary researchers have discovered that the more theologically conservative church members are, the less likely they are to show any interest in saving our planet from what is certainly an impending ecological holocaust. We are going to have to ask ourselves why. This is an especially important question since the most often quoted verse in the Bible, John 3:16, tells us clearly that

"God so loved the *world* that He gave His only begotten Son" to rescue it from the effects of sin and corruption.

There are those who try to escape from what this verse has to say to us about the environment by claiming that when the Gospel of John tells us that "God so loved the world," the word *world* only refers to human beings. Their particular interpretation of John 3:16 implies that God has no deep and abiding concern with what happens to other living creatures or to our physical environment. The salvation of God, they claim, is only meant for *homo sapiens*.

This twisting of John 3:16 belies the fact that in the original Greek, the word for *world* is the Greek word *cosmos*. And as any lexicon makes quite clear, the Greek word *cosmos* refers to anything and everything that is in the universe, including the animals, flowers, insects, and fish—God loves them all. It also includes the land and the oceans and the air we breathe. Of course, God loves us humans most of all. But we must not allow His great love for us to obliterate the fact that He loves all of His creation.

To be a Christian is to be concerned for this planet and for those creatures, great and small, which inhabit it along with us. As we shall see, faithfulness to the Word of God should make us "green Christians"—those whose concern for the environment arises out of biblical imperatives.

Green Christians remind the rest of the church that God, after He created this world, looked on all that He had created and called it "good" (Genesis 1:31). Furthermore, they declare that this same God is brokenhearted over what has happened to us and to our world because we sinfully abused His gift of creation. They know that it was God's heartfelt concern for us and for planet earth that moved Him to send His Son into history with the mission to rescue His cosmos and to make it new again (Revelation 21:5). Green Christians are those whose hearts resonate with the heart of God and share a burden with Him for His sick and dying creation.

GREEN CHRISTIANS AND SOCIAL JUSTICE

Over the last three decades, many evangelical Christians have awakened to the fact that the call for social justice lies at the very heart of the gospel. Without buying into the Marxist tendencies inherent in some of the liberation theologies, they have come, nevertheless, to recognize that the God described in the Scripture is a God who is at work in the world abolishing all forms of oppression. They have learned that our God is a God who expresses the truth that makes people free. That which prevents anyone from realizing what God wants him or her to be is considered to be sin. And anything or anybody who exercises destructive power in the world is looked upon as evil. This relatively new breed of socially conscious, theologically conservative, evangelical Christian often becomes involved with issues and concerns which have heretofore been considered to be part of the politically liberal agenda. A newly acquired commitment to biblically prescribed social justice has made these people intolerant of intolerance.

They stand opposed to any form of racism and have been a strong voice against the apartheid that has plagued South Africa. They identify with many, though by no means all, of the concerns of the feminist movement. They have joined in the attack on homophobia, and they have argued against political and economic policies that seem to discriminate against the poor.

Most recently, these socially conscious, evangelical Christians have taken up the cause of saving the environment from destruction. They have found much that seems "right" to them in the program and activities of organizations such as Greenpeace. They regard with increasing respect people like Cleveland Armory and Alex Pacheo who championed the animal rights movement.

One of the primary reasons for this developing involvement in efforts to preserve God's creation lies in the growing awareness that those who are most prone to suffer the consequences of environmental irresponsibility are the poor. If changes in the climate and erosion of the soil through deforestation result in diminished food production, the poor will go hungry. As the temperature on the earth's surface edges upward, the poor will have no air conditioning to make life bearable. And, as a shortage of the world's drinkable water supply becomes more and more acute, the poor will go thirsty.

DESTRUCTIVE CHAIN REACTION

Already the poor and weak are suffering the consequences of the exploitation of nature. In the Amazon, the precious rain forest is being systematically destroyed. Every minute a parcel of the jungle, the size of a football field, is leveled. Every year an area of the jungle, the size of the state of Massachusetts, is devastated. The reason is simple. More land is needed for grazing cattle. As the annual consumption rate of beef soars in nations like

Japan, Germany, and the United States, cattlemen raze the forests to make room for raising cattle.

The rain forest of the Amazon has been the home of preliterate tribes who lack the means to defend themselves against the encroachment of "civilized" peoples who want their land. These poor and defenseless indigenous people are no match for those who use guns and tractors to take away and to destroy their natural habitat. So innocent people are pushed off their land, lose their homes, and are driven to extinction, all to ensure the beef supply for people who would be a whole lot healthier if they didn't eat so much of it.

Believe it or not, there is an even worse consequence of the devastation of the Amazon rain forest—an ongoing famine in Africa. In the Sahel region of Africa, climate changes are making drought and famine inevitable. The rain that makes life viable in this part of the world comes from the rain forests in Brazil. The moisture from the jungle forms rain clouds that float across the Atlantic to fall upon the parched soil of such countries as Mauritania, Senegal, and Mali. But, because the rain forests have been depleted, the rain clouds, so essential for the survival of life in the Sahel, have become increasingly rare. Less rain has resulted in more than a drought; it has created a permanent climate change in the Sahel—a climate change that will mean starvation and death for millions of Africans. It's all connected, you see. We eat hamburgers here; they cut down the jungle in Brazil, and there's a climate change that kills people in Africa.

The chief of a nomadic tribe living along the south bank of the Senegal River told me that for centuries his people herded sheep and goats from place to place throughout the semiarid region. But things changed. The animals died. The chief said that his people were hungry and despairing about the future.

The chief and his people had known many droughts over the years, but he knew that what was happening now was more than a drought. Somehow he knew that this was a climate change. He knew that his people, who had survived centuries of droughts, would soon be no more. He told me with a deep sadness, which defies description, that he was facing the beginning of the end of the history of his tribe.

Something had gone wrong with nature. The elements turned against him, and he did not know why. Drawing from his Muslim beliefs, all he could say to me was that this must be happening because, according to Allah, "It is written." He knows nothing of the growing appetite for red meat among Westernized peoples that compels the clearing of the rain forests. He has not heard that the jungle, which once produced the desperately needed rain, is now being systematically destroyed. All he knows is the wind does not feel the same when it blows on his face, and the Senegal River has changed. Rivers do not talk to me, but this chief told me that the river had spoken to him and said that it was dying.

The chief told me that the young men, hoping to find jobs, had already abandoned the tribe and had migrated to the lights of Dakar. He told me how the elders of the tribe sat for hours discussing what was happening while trying to discern Allah's will. He showed me his people, and I saw women trying to nurse their infants from dried up breasts. I saw children with stomachs swollen from malnutrition. There was the feeling of death in the air.

I wondered why the chief and his people stayed out there on the parched land. What little water was available was being pumped to the capital city so that residents would have enough to drink. Keeping people in the capital relatively comfortable was essential to prevent an uprising.

I asked the chief, "Why don't you leave this land and go to live in the city as your sons have done? Why do you stay out here where everything is becoming a desert?"

After a poignant silence, he spoke. "Have you been to the city? Have you seen how people live there? Have you seen what happens to the women in the city? If you have, you will understand why we have decided to die out here in the wilderness."

Some of us say that what is happening to this tribe is sin. For the sake of justice, the rain forest must be saved. It is not right in the eyes of God that some people should eat what they do not need and live in such a way as to cause people in far and distant lands to suffer. If justice is to roll down for those who cannot defend themselves against the power of the rich nations of the earth, the people of God must try to put an end to this oppression. We must try to save the rain forests in Brazil.

But you don't even have to be a Christian committed to social justice to get upset over the destruction of the rain forests of Brazil. Plain, old-fashioned self-interest will do it.

Consider the fact that the destruction of the Brazilian rain forest is in all probability destroying some special forms of plant life that hold the cures to some of the most terrible diseases and sicknesses in the world today. Most of us have paid little attention to the fact that many of the medicines we use in the treatment of illnesses are compounds derived from plants. Plants develop unique properties which cannot be duplicated with chemicals in laboratories. Often special plants are the only sources of the essential organic pharmaceuticals, the wonder drugs hailed by those who practice medicine. As we destroy the jungles of Brazil, we know we are destroying thousands of rare plants that have as yet undetermined curative properties for many of the sicknesses that torture us, our families, and our friends. There is no way of telling whether or not, at this very moment, the cure for cancer or for AIDS is being wiped from the face of the earth.

Consider the story told by Jay D. Hair, president of the National Wildlife Federation:

> About four years ago . . . my older daughter Whitney was very ill with cancer. She literally came within a few days of death. She is here today, and she is a beautiful, fourteen-year-old, healthy, completely cured young lady. Why? The drug that saved her life was derived from a plant called the rosy periwinkle. The rosy periwinkle was a plant native to the island country of Madagascar. The irony of this story is that 90 percent of the forested area of Madagascar has been destroyed. One hundred percent of all native habitat of the rosy periwinkle is gone forever. And just at a time when we're learning about the marvels of biotechnology. We are losing entire genetic stocks of wild living resources at a time when we're learning about the potential medical marvels of some of these plants, like the one used to cure my daughter. We are destroying them and their potential values forever. This is a tragedy with incredible consequences to the future of global societies.

3

BEATING
A BUM RAP

Putting the Blame
for the Disaster on the Guilty

*T*he Calvinists seem to get blamed for everything. There are psychologists who claim that the Calvinist-based beliefs of the Puritans are responsible for all of our sex hang-ups. There are sociologists who claim that Calvinism is a belief system that has turned too many of us into workaholics. And now some environmentalists are taking shots at the heirs of the Geneva Reformer.

In 1967, Lynn White published an article in *Science* magazine that blamed Protestant Christianity and, more specifically, Calvinism, for the orientation toward nature that has led to ecological disaster.[1]

There is no doubt that John Calvin—the prime creator of the reformed theology that has so strongly influenced the development of Protestant Christianity in the industrialized, capitalistic societies of the Western world—had what might be called "a utilitarian view of nature." Put simply, the only value that nature has, so far as Calvin was concerned, is in the use that we humans might find for it. God, according to Calvin, created nature essentially for our use and enjoyment. Calvin wrote in his commentary on the book of Genesis:

> We infer what was the end for which all things were created; namely, that none of the conveniences and necessaries of life might be wanting to men. In the very order of the creation the paternal solicitude of God for man is conspicuous, because he furnished the world with all things needful, and even with an immense profusion of wealth, before he formed man. Thus man was rich before he was born.[2]

Using such passages, interpreters of Calvin have claimed that Calvin saw nothing inherently sacred about nature and believed that there was nothing essentially spiritual about animals. Most subsequent theologians generally agree that Calvin taught that the other resources of nature exist to enhance the lives of human beings. From Calvin's utilitarian point of view, apart from supplying humans with what they need (for example, food), the rest of nature has no real purpose at all.

Lynn White contends that this kind of thinking has led to the justification of an almost indiscriminate exploitation of nature. In the context of a Calvinistic worldview, animals can be slaughtered, and entire species can be exterminated, so long as such killing meets some real or imagined human need. Forests can be wiped off the face of the earth if it is proved humanly desirable. Armed with this kind of thinking, we can mine minerals until they disappear, and we can dump atomic waste into the seas to our hearts' content. All of these practices, and more, according to White, are Calvin's fault or at least the fault of his followers.

However, I contend that contrary to White's understanding, Calvin had more than a utilitarian view of nature. I must point out that in that same commentary on Genesis to which White refers in his article, Calvin also urges us to be good stewards of God's creation. While Calvin may tell us, in accord with his understanding of the Bible, that we have the right to subdue nature and exercise dominance over it, he also tells us to assume responsibility for God's creation. Stewardship over creation means that we should treat creation with the same loving care as Jesus would if He were in our place.

Those of us who have followed Calvin's teachings have tended to pick up on this stewardship theme. What is more, to some degree, we have applied the biblical teachings about stewardship to our relationship with nature. For instance, when we read the parable on the talents, we readily conclude that Jesus is giving the directions we need to approach our physical and biological environments in a way that is responsible and godly:

> For the kingdom of heaven is like a man traveling to a far country, who called his own servants and delivered his goods to them. And to one he gave five talents, to another two, and to another one; to each according to his own ability; and immediately he went on a journey. Then he who had received the five talents went and traded with them, and made another five talents. And likewise he who had received two gained two more also. But he who had received one went and dug in the ground, and hid his lord's money. After a long

time the lord of those servants came and settled accounts with them.

So he who had received five talents came and brought five other talents, saying, "Lord you delivered to me five talents; look, I have gained five more talents besides them." His lord said to him, "Well done, good and faithful servant; you were faithful over a few things, I will make you ruler over many things. Enter into the joy of your lord." He also who had received two talents came and said, "Lord, you delivered to me two talents; look, I have gained two more talents besides them." His lord said to him, "Well done, good and faithful servant; you have been faithful over a few things, I will make you ruler over many things. Enter into the joy of your lord."

Then he who had received the one talent came and said, "Lord, I knew you would be a hard man, reaping where you have not sown, and gathering where you have not scattered seed. And I was afraid, and went and hid your talent in the ground. Look, there you have what is yours."

But his lord answered and said to him, "You wicked and lazy servant, you knew that I reap where I have not sown, and gather where I have not scattered seed. So you ought to have deposited my money with the bankers, and at my coming I would have received back my own with interest. Therefore take the talent from him, and give it to him who has ten talents.

"For to everyone who has, more will be given, and he will have abundance; but from him who does not have, even what he has will be taken away. And cast the unprofitable servant into the outer darkness. There will be weeping and gnashing of teeth." (Matthew 25:14–30)

Calvinists understand this text to mean that we are to take what God has provided, nurture it, care for it, and enable it to produce more than might be otherwise expected. Irrational abuse of nature is not permitted. Ignoring our responsibility to protect nature and failing to nurture nature to abundance are clearly sins. According to the Scriptures, as interpreted by the followers of Calvin, we are not only to preserve nature, but we are to make it even more beautiful and fruitful than it was when we received it from God.

It is that kind of joyful, satisfying, caring relationship that God wills for each of us to have with His creation. God, according to Calvin's thinking, wants us to become partners with Him in making His creation increasingly beautiful and fruitful. He expects us to guard it and deliver it up to Him in glorious, renewed form at the end of history.

Unfortunately, not all of those who have followed in the Calvinistic train have been responsible stewards. A few years back, the secretary of the interior—a man with strong religious beliefs formed under the influence of Calvin's admonition to "subdue" nature—thought that getting cheap oil out of the ground was more important than preserving nature's beauty and balance. In this case, his strong commitment to Christ did not lead him to be kindly disposed to green Christianity. Instead, he advocated off-shore oil drilling in spite of the hazards. He believed it was important to satisfy our exorbitant lust for cheap energy even if it was ecologically dangerous.

THE REAL CULPRIT—SCIENCE

In an ironic twist to Lynn White's article in *Science* magazine, the real culprit in the obscene exploitation of the environment is not religion at all. Instead, a careful look at the ideas that have molded contemporary attitudes toward nature will show that science itself is responsible. The real culprit was the outgrowth of the Enlightenment and the scientific approach to life. The philosophical approach of the hero of the Enlightenment, Rene Descartes, probably did the most damage.

Descartes established for the intellectual world the idea that the universe was a gigantic machine guided by scientifically discoverable laws. According to Descartes, there was nothing mystical or spiritual about nature. Whereas Aristotle taught that everything in nature had a subjective side (i.e., even rocks had feelings), Descartes taught that nature was without spirit or soul and that it was nothing more than a gigantic machine. Consequently, myths and beliefs suggesting animals had personal consciousness were no longer popular. Such a "rational" approach to things eventually led to the kind of infamous statement made by Joshua Lederferg:

> Now we can define man. He is six feet of a particular molecular sequence of carbon, hydrogen, oxygen, nitrogen, and phosphorous atoms.

The new science spawned by Descartes challenged those who believed that human beings were created in the image of God. And it gave no credence at all to claims that the rest of nature deserved reverence and loving care.

The humanism that followed Descartes' philosophy only made matters worse. According to this new humanism, human beings became the measure of all things and the center of all concerns. Intellectuals defined *humans* as the supreme beings of the universe. God and the values that He posited for humanity and the lesser creatures on the phylogenetic scale were considered the figments of prescientific superstitions. To the heirs of Descartes, human beings were all that mattered.

This human-centered thinking ruined everything. For those who followed this new rationalism, nothing had a spiritual quality anymore, and nothing but human beings had anything that could be called ultimate value. Those who blame Christianity for diminishing the sacredness of the world should take an honest look at the scientific rationalism that followed the Cartesian intellectual revolution.

When students of the cultures of Native Americans read a book such as *Black Elk Speaks,* they often blame biblical religion and the attitudes generated by the Judeo-Christian tradition for the loss of the awe and reverence people once had for the natural world. But I believe the sense that animals, flowers, and trees have a spiritual value, which makes them worthy of care, was not lost because of a worldview generated by biblical Christianity. Actually, Christians worship a Jesus who could talk to the wind and the waves (Matthew 8:23–27), who considered lilies to be more filled with "glory" than anything we humans might create (Matthew 6:28–29), and who is a spiritual presence through whom everything in the universe is held together (Colossians 1:16–17). The preachers of biblical revelation, even those in the Protestant tradition, are not the culprits behind the loss of spiritual mystery about the world. It is those hard-nosed scientific rationalists who have taken the life out of everything. They are the ones to blame.

Do you remember when you had to dissect a frog in biology class?

Do you remember how the teacher told you not to get emotional or let your imagination run away with you?

You were not to ask yourself questions like, *How does the poor frog feel about all of this?*

"This is science!" commanded your teacher. "You are supposed to be objective and not let your feelings enter into what you are doing!"

Think back to all of that, and then ask whether it was what you learned in Sunday school or what you learned in science class that prepared you to be unfeeling about nature. Ask yourself honestly, was it religion or science that taught you to view nature as devoid of sacredness and available to be "used" as you saw fit?

Max Weber, the famous father of German sociology, contended that because of scientific rationalization, man has become disenchanted with his world. Erich Fromm, one of the prime figures in the Frankfurt School of Social Science, makes a similar point in his writings in psychoanalysis.

Fromm said human beings, under the influence of science, have undergone a process of emotional separation from the rest of nature, and therefore, we no longer believe we can have any kind of feeling of "oneness" with nature. Even Karl Marx, the sociologist who reduced everything in time and history to material forces, bemoaned the fact that humanity, under the influence of science, had become alienated from the rest of nature and that people had become strangers in their own world.

None of these social scientists considered themselves to be religious. And in the case of Marx, the more blame that could be dumped on religion the better. Yet all of them blamed science, not Calvinism, for the negative and "unspiritual" attitudes people had toward nature.

The loss of mystery and awe about nature and the sense that we alone in all of creation have subjective feelings, these have contributed to the mindset that accepts the destruction of the environment as a necessary evil. Science has brought on a loss of emotional affinity, and that has caused all the trouble.

Only people who do not consider the feelings of animals can kill them for fun. Only those who sense nothing "holy" about the forests and the plants can destroy them with little concern. Only those who do not sense the stars and galaxies declaring the glory of God can be indifferent to the pollution that hides them from view.

Recently a friend was berating me over my views on hunting. He said, "Your problem, Tony, is that you saw the movie *Bambi.* You think that every little buck and doe has a personality. Your problem is that you believe animals feel what we feel and react like we react. Well, you're wrong. There is an infinite difference between humans and animals. It's crazy to project onto animals the emotions and reactions that belong to us."

As he spoke, I wondered, *How does he know? What does he grasp about the subjective feelings of the deer that he blows away with his rifle? By what means does he come to such certainty about what goes on in the consciousness of animals?* Limited though it might be, perhaps there is some likeness between the sufferings of animals as they face death and what we feel in the same situation. And besides, who but God knows what animals really feel?

This much is certain: Animals feel pain. Even those heirs of Descartes, who view nature in the most mechanical of ways, know that animals feel pain. Insects also suffer. Research demonstrates that even worms feel pain. Worms, which are among the lowliest creatures in God's creation, secrete certain chemicals to diminish their suffering when they are hurt. Worms feel!

What I know about Jesus may be very limited, but this is certain: Jesus knows the pain that His creatures suffer. The Jesus I met through Scripture would never inflict pain if it were not absolutely necessary. And I am convinced Jesus would never make hurting animals into a sport. Killing for food is one thing, but killing for the fun of it is something else. Jesus demonstrated more reverence for life than that.

I know this may sound a bit off-the-wall, but there is increasing evidence that even flowers "feel." Tests give evidence that when roses are surrounded by loving conversation, they bloom with brilliance. But when anger fills the air and hateful talk surrounds them, they tend to wither and die.

I know there are some who will write off such statements as imagination gone wild or fantasy thinking. But before they do, they should go to the library and read what the research has discovered.

THE BIRTH OF
A NEW KIND OF SCIENCE

Over the past few years, a new science has been born— a more humble science that does not claim to know what it cannot prove. This science is ready to admit there may be subjective feelings in nature beyond our ability to explore. The new science challenges the cold, hard rationalism stimulated by the philosophy of Descartes. The results are beginning to change the way we look at nature. In the new emerging worldview that is becoming more and more a part of contemporary consciousness, the old arrogance that claimed, "Man is the measure of all things" is being eclipsed. In its place, a new view of nature is coming into play; religion is not being blamed so much as it is being welcomed for providing a different kind of knowledge—knowledge that is beyond the scope of scientific findings. Instead of blaming religion for all that is wrong in the world, the new children of the sciences are recognizing there is more to the universe than meets the eye.

From the time of Albert Einstein on, even physicists have been aware there is, what one writer called, a *mysterium tremendum* about the universe. Physicists are no longer as apt to blame those who believe in spirituality for the ecological mess. And they are much less likely to contend that religious attitudes, generated by the biblical God-given instructions to Adam and Eve "to subdue the earth" and to dominate it for their own purposes, lie behind the ecological disaster we face. Instead, these physicists increasingly recognize that their own former rationalistic approach to nature is responsible.

A world without God is not viewed with a sense of awe. A universe in which His presence is not felt is doomed to abuse. Such a world is primarily the creation of science. The theologians did not produce the chemicals that we have pumped into the air. Priests and rabbis did not create the plastics that clog our rivers and choke the dolphins. It was science—or more specifically, a particular kind of science.

The science generated by Descartes and those other children of the Enlightenment is to blame. The rationalistic approach to nature fostered in the Enlightenment did the damage. This approach taught us to use whatever we could find in our environment to further our own selfish interests without regard to the consequences. It led us to forsake "creation-care," and to abandon the stewardship which God asked us to exercise when He entrusted this planet into our hands.

Having tried to defend Calvin against White's "bum rap," I think it is far more important to acknowledge that the real cause of our problem lies elsewhere. In the final analysis, it accomplishes very little for scientists and Calvinistic clerics to point fingers at each other. Deep down inside, I think we all know the truth. And that truth is that there is something radically wrong with human nature. There is an innate sinfulness at the core of our being that lies at the base of all of our troubles.

Greed in the human heart drives us to use everything and everybody around us to get what we want. There is a selfishness within us that makes us seek to gratify our own wants regardless of who suffers.

This perversity allows you and me to participate in the destruction of the rain forests and cause suffering for millions in order to satisfy our own appetite for beef. We disregard the consequences for others as we drive automobiles that pollute the air. We say nothing when our garbage gets dumped into the sea. The condition called "original sin," which, ironically enough, was best described by Calvin, is what makes us unwilling to adopt a more socially and environmentally responsible life-style.

In the end, this theological explanation of what has gone wrong in the world may make the most sense. And furthermore, a theologically prescribed cure to our environmental crisis may be our best hope for the future.

Repentance rather than recrimination is what we need. Repentance instead of finger-pointing is the beginning of the answer.

There are signs of hope. Pope John Paul II talks of repenting "the inconsiderate forms of domination" that have plagued the planet in the modern era. He talks of a new epoch of stewardship in which the kingdom of God might be expressed through the saving of creation from destruction.[3]

The church may yet raise up prophets in our day who will teach us all how to weep over what we have done to God's creation. And perhaps these prophets coming out of the church will be joined by a new breed of prophets coming out of the scientific community. Perhaps together they can call us to a repentance based on what the Bible teaches about our responsibility to be good stewards of creation as well as on the empirical evidence of our impending ecological catastrophe.

Instead of calling us names, spokespersons for the scientific community are beginning to acknowledge that there is an increasing sensitivity to environmental concerns within the church. Many in the scientific community seem ready to acknowledge that there is, stirring within the church, an awareness of what we, who have been poor stewards of God's creation, should be doing to rescue this dying planet. More and more empirical rationalists are becoming aware that Christians are coming up with plans of action that offer the hope of rescuing an environment that is perishing—a rescue effort based on creating a sense of commitment to care for what is dying in this fallen world.

A colleague of mine at Eastern College, biologist Dr. Joseph Sheldon, has compiled an impressive bibliography of theological writings on nature. These writings integrate the insights of the field of biology with the truths of Scripture in order to create an ecologically responsible value system. Sheldon gives ample evidence that Christianity and science can come together to facilitate the kind of change of consciousness that will help us to be environmentally concerned.[4]

Certainly, mainline Protestant denominational leaders have been trying to foster a new awareness of ecological issues. Under the influence of the delegates from Africa, the World Council of Churches, meeting in Nairobi in 1975, saw the need to develop a theology of nature. The Africans who were not as heavily influenced by the ideas of the Enlightenment, so prevalent in industrialized nations, made it clear that holistic Christianity must have a keen understanding and sense of responsibility for living creatures as well as for the nonliving elements of God's creation. Their insistence that the World Council of Churches focus on nature has been the impetus for a flurry of discussion and ecclesiastical resolution that is giving new direction to the church. Currently in mainline Protestant denominations, it is difficult to go to conventions or conclaves where environmental issues are not the subject of sermons and seminars.

With the motivation to be good stewards of God's creation provided by a biblical faith, the sensitivity to nature created by an infilling of the Holy Spirit, and an awareness of what needs to be done provided by scientific research, there would seem to be, at the very least, the possibility for a united and ultimately successful effort to save the earth from destruction.

4

WHAT IN THE WORLD IS GOD DOING?

A Look at the Thinking of the Eastern Orthodox Church

I was sitting in the waiting area just prior to boarding a plane in Norfolk, Virginia, when I noticed a young man working the crowd. He was moving from person to person asking each person in turn if he or she was "saved."

I have always admired people with that kind of zeal for evangelism. But I have always felt a bit ashamed, in the face of such bold witnesses for the gospel, that I am sometimes so reluctant to tell others about Jesus. That young man may have been a bit obnoxious, but his sincerity was obvious.

I watched with mixed feelings as he lay out the way of salvation to anyone who would listen. Eventually he got to an elderly black man who was sitting right next to me. The man was slouched in his seat; his head was bowed in sleep with his chin resting on his chest.

The young evangelist came and stood directly in front of him, cleared his throat, and as the old man slowly opened his eyes, inquired, "Excuse me, sir! But are you saved?"

The old man answered softly, "I am."

The intense inquisitor shot back with a second question. "Can you tell me exactly *when* you were saved?"

"Well, not exactly," was the answer. "You see," he went on deliberately, "it was about two thousand years ago." Then, allowing a smile to cross his face, he added, "I just found out about it recently."

What a wonderful answer! The death of Christ on the cross two thousand years ago *is* what saves each and every one of us. That He died for you and me is fact. It only remains for each of us to acknowledge that good news by calling Him Lord of our lives. If we try to reduce the message of salvation to its most essential propositional truths, we probably cannot do much better than the now-famous *Four Spiritual Laws* outlined so clearly by Bill Bright of Campus Crusade.

1. God loves you and has a wonderful plan for your life.

2. Man is sinful and separated from God. Thus he cannot know and experience God's love and plan for his life.

3. Jesus Christ is God's only provision for man's sin. Through Him you can know and experience God's love and plan for your life.

4. We must individually receive Jesus Christ as Savior and Lord; then we can know and experience God's love and plan for our lives.[1]

But as effective as these four spiritual laws are in helping people become Christians, they do not tell the whole story. Just when we think we have the story of salvation down pat, along comes some new way of looking at what Christ accomplished on the cross that sets our minds spinning with a fresh sense of awe. No wonder the writer of the Gospel of John wrote:

> And there are also many other things that Jesus did, which if they were written one by one, I suppose that even the world itself could not contain the books that would be written. Amen. (John 21:25)

As you might suspect, all of this leads to the introduction of a new way of thinking about the cross that has a great deal to do with the way we look at nature. This new way of thinking comes to us from a source we in the nations of the West have seldom taken seriously. It comes from some churches that, to most of us, seem strange and perhaps even alien to the Christianity with which we are familiar. I am referring to the beliefs of the Eastern Orthodox churches.

These Christians from Greece, Eastern Europe, and that array of countries which were once a part of the Soviet Union have things to teach us about what Christ accomplished in His death and resurrection that few of us have ever considered. And what they can teach us is so relevant to our understanding of what God is trying to do in this world that we cannot ignore it.

SALVATION IS BIGGER THAN WE IMAGINED

While our Orthodox brothers and sisters readily affirm the good news that salvation for us as individuals was made possible through Christ's death, they go on to say that there is much more to the cross and resurrection. They preach that what Christ accomplished two thousand years ago was not only deliverance from the consequences of sin in our personal lives, but also deliverance for the rest of creation from what Satan had done to it. It goes something like this:

5. Before there was ever a heaven or an earth—before "the beginning"—Satan, the most powerful of all the angels, led a rebellion against God. Satan was jealous of God's power and wanted it for himself.

6. God responded to Satan's rebellion by casting him and the angels who had joined him (one third of the angelic host) out of heaven.

7. Since Satan's fall, he and his followers have been at work perverting and polluting all that God created. Before Adam and Eve were ever created, Satan worked to create havoc throughout creation.

8. One of the consequences of Satan's work is that the evolutionary process has gone haywire. That is why we have mosquitoes, germs, viruses, etc. God did not create these evils. They evolved because Satan perverted the developmental forces at work in nature.

9. Behind all that Satan did to nature and to the human race was the desire to deny God a creation and persons that would worship Him. Satan has

always been jealous of God, and he's committed to keeping any glory from being given to God.

10. God wills the rescuing of His creation from what Satan has done to it. He wills that all creatures, great and small, and all of nature, animate and inanimate, worship Him and glorify Him forever.

11. To accomplish this rescue and deliverance, God commissioned His Son to do battle with Satan. Two thousand years ago His Son became a man and in this "weak" form confronted the Evil One. Satan, working through the principalities, powers, and rulers of this world, was seemingly able to defeat the Christ.

12. Then, three days later, Jesus reversed everything! He rose from the dead. He shook off the chains of sin and death, broke the power of Satan, and became *Christus Victor*.

13. When Jesus conquered Satan, He not only provided for our deliverance from eternal death, He also initiated the freeing of nature from the evil effects of Satan's work. The ultimate result of the work of Christ is that all of nature and all of humanity will be giving God glory and worshiping Him throughout all eternity.

A SALVATION THEORY THAT EXPLAINS A LOT

What the Orthodox Church teaches explains a great deal of that which troubled Protestants and Catholics in the Western world when they did theology. For instance, it explains why there are so many "mean" characteristics in nature and assures us that God didn't create them.

There is a horrible violence evident throughout the animal kingdom. Every time those *National Geographic* films about the lives of animals are shown on television, I tend to cringe. I have a hard time viewing the viciousness that seems to be part and parcel of the everyday lives of animals. I am overtaken by morbid fascination as I watch wolves scout out and bring down their prey. But then I have to look away as they tear apart an innocent lamb. The specter of hawks swooping down to rip open the necks of mice and squirrels leaves me with a very queasy feeling. And those scenes of adorable lion cubs with bloody faces chewing at the carcasses of deer killed by their mothers creates in me a fascinated kind of revulsion.

Through it all, I experience a painful twinge that tells me something has gone wrong out there in the jungle; God did not create the animals to live this way. There is within me a haunting but difficult-to-explain sense that God never meant His creation to be so filled with viciousness and suffering.

More and more I come to the conclusion that the seemingly sinister creatures that sneak up on their victims for the kill are reflecting a perversity that is contrary to the will of the One who gave them life. There is a sense I have that, as beautiful as nature may appear to be, there is something evil about it.

CHILDREN KNOW

I find refreshingly honest the fears children express when they walk in the forest. For them, the tall trees do not create within them a sense of security. The sound of nature does not give a sensation of safety or peace. Children take their steps with caution and act as though there are dangerous and ugly creatures lurking in wait for them. Nature does not seem friendly to little children. We adults must constantly reassure them there is nothing to worry about and that nothing out there is going to hurt them. But still they are not so sure. We have to train children not to be afraid. But the bravado that eventually allows them to whistle a happy tune on their way to grandmother's house on the other side of the woods usually masks a certain lingering hesitancy within them.

It seems these little ones are not quite as sure of themselves as they would like us to believe. Children resonate to the fairy tales that tell them the woods are filled with big bad wolves and witches. Perhaps this is because children have already felt the presence of these threatening creatures when they have gone for walks with big people. Certainly, going into the forest alone is, for children, one of the most threatening of all adventures.

Do children who have not yet been taught to repress their feelings grasp a certain truth about the forest to which big people no longer pay attention? Are they aware of something the rest of us have forced ourselves to ignore? Is it just childish imagination that causes them to be frightened and tell us "I want to go home"?

Furthermore, I often wonder if the reaction of children to being in the forest is not somewhat akin to what the animals themselves constantly feel. The rabbit frozen in its path, the wildcat with its hunched back, and even the rattlesnake poised for its strike all reek of fear. Is it just a projection of my childish emotions onto the animal kingdom or is the natural condition of nature fraught with a sense of being in danger?

But there is something more than fear that comes from any communion I have with nature. There is also a certain sadness. Whenever I walk in the woods alone, I inevitably pick up a strange but certain sense of melancholia. The birds, I notice, sing in a minor key, and their songs stir within me hard-to-explain feelings of remorse. Even the sounds of the crickets and the buzzing of the bees seem to give off an eeriness that, if I let it, create a queer pervading pathos in my bones. Is it just my imagination or *is* there a feeling of sorrow I pick up when I go into the woods?

I believe nature is moaning in pain. I believe that my sense of nature's suffering may be something generated by the Holy Spirit. The Bible teaches that it is the work of the Holy Spirit in my life that creates this awareness of nature's suffering within me. That, of course, is what the apostle Paul poetically said in his epistle to the Romans:

> For we know that the whole creation groans and labors with birth pangs together until now. And not only they, but we also who have the firstfruits of the Spirit, even we ourselves groan within ourselves, eagerly waiting for the adoption, the redemption of our body. (Romans 8:22–23)

Nature really does suffer. The animals really are afraid. The sounds I hear in the forest really are groanings. It is not just my imagination. There really is suffering out there, and the sensitivity I have to the moanings and groanings of nature is really the prompting of the Holy Spirit urging me to respond.

What the teachings of Eastern Orthodoxy explain is *why* nature is in this sad condition. The Evil One, they claim, has permeated all of nature and has perverted it. As the creatures in nature evolve, they do so in ways that are evil and cruel. They become creatures that bring sickness, disease, and death to every corner of the globe. Through a perverted process of evolution, a mean and threatening spirit has become omnipresent in nature. It was not always this way. This is the work of Satan who started his work long before Adam and Eve ever arrived on the scene.

WORSHIP IS THE GOAL

This theory of salvation also gives a whole new understanding of the purpose of salvation. With Eastern Orthodox Christians, salvation is not as "human centered" as it is in the theologies of the West. They explain for us that when Jesus died on the cross He did not do it just to provide passage for people like you and me to heaven when we die. He also did it, they claim, to restore everything and every creature in the entire cosmos so that all can worship God. Glorifying God is the purpose of Christ's work. Worship is the ultimate meaning of salvation. What Jesus has done and is doing still is transforming all creatures (especially those of us who were created in His image) so that our greatest joy will come in worshiping God.

I remember with fondness a story told by C. S. Lewis in his intriguing book, *The Great Divorce*. In it, everybody who dies goes to heaven. The only people who end up in hell are those who do not like heaven and do not want to stay there. They, of course, are "the unsaved." They are the ones who want themselves to be the center of attention and who get no pleasure at all in the glory going to God, which is what heaven is all about.

In Lewis's "make believe" story, there is a bus that makes regular runs to hell. Those who have refused to be made into persons who delight in worshiping the Lord line up to board it. Such self-centered persons willingly choose to go to that dark place where the worship of God does not exist.

Not only do Eastern Orthodox Christians stress worshiping God, they also provide us an awesome hope for the future. They assure us that this world will not be abandoned by God. The heavens and the earth will not be left to the destructive exploitations of selfish people. The world will not end with a bang or a whimper. Instead, as those in Eastern Orthodoxy remind us:

> . . . and by Him to reconcile all things to Himself, by Him, whether things on earth or things in heaven, having made peace through the blood of His cross. (Colossians 1:20)

Eastern Orthodox Christians promise us that He will make all things new (Revelation 21:5). They declare the good news that the devastating work of Satan will be reversed. And they preach that the pollution and ecological destruction brought on by our careless life-styles and greed will not only be ended, but the earth will be healed and its full beauty restored. Instead of being prophets of doom, they become prophets who echo the message of Isaiah:

> The wolf also shall dwell with the lamb,
> The leopard shall lie down
>   with the young goat,
> The calf and the young lion and
>   the fatling together;
> And a little child shall lead them.
> The cow and the bear shall graze;

Their young ones shall lie down together;
And the lion shall eat straw like the ox.
The nursing child shall play
    by the cobra's hole,
And the weaned child shall put his hand
    in the viper's den.
They shall not hurt nor destroy
    in all My holy mountain,
For the earth shall be full of the knowledge
    of the LORD
As the waters cover the sea.

(Isaiah 11:6–9)

All of this is such a contrast to what I grew up believing. I thought my Bible-believing church had let me in on what would happen in the last days. The message I got in my Sunday school lessons was that the world would get worse and worse until it would get so bad that the Lord would have to destroy it. Actually, word of how bad things were getting was welcome news, because I had been led to believe that the "signs of the times" were evils and destructions that seemed to be increasing all around me with every passing day. I'm not sure why we thought this message of doom was "preaching the gospel," since gospel means "good news."

Over and against such blatant pessimism is the good news echoed by our Eastern Orthodox friends. They affirm that things *are* getting worse but that the kingdom of God is also growing. They want us to remember God is at work restoring the ruined world to its ordained magnificence. Both kingdoms are growing up side by side:

Another parable He put forth to them, saying: "The kingdom of heaven is like a man who sowed good seed in his field; but while men slept, his enemy came and sowed tares among the wheat and went his way. But when the grain had sprouted and produced a crop, the tares also appeared. So the servants of the owner came and said to him, 'Sir, did you not sow good seed in your field? How then does it have tares?' He said to them, 'An enemy has done this.' The servants said to him, 'Do you want us then to go and gather them up?' But he said, 'No, lest while you gather up the tares you also uproot the wheat with them. Let both grow together until the harvest, and at the time of harvest I will say to the reapers, "First gather together tares and bind them in bundles to burn them, but gather the wheat into my barn."'" (Matthew 13:24–30)

What Eastern Orthodoxy tells us is that these two conflicting kingdoms will continue to grow until Christ returns. They claim the Second Coming will doom the kingdom of darkness and bring to the final triumph the kingdom of God. The end is renewal! The end is restoration! The end is a new heaven and a new earth!

BUT THERE'S STILL A PROBLEM

While the decisive battle with the powers of darkness and death has been won, we all realize that the pain in nature and the suffering of both animals and people continues. The rivers are still being polluted. The soil is still being eroded. And the atmosphere is still being eaten away. Satan's presence, the presence of the "great destroyer," is still everywhere to be seen.

That's because we live between God's D-Day and His V-Day. We must grasp the good news that we are now dealing with a defeated enemy whose eventual destruction has been assured. Even as we see the hand of the Evil One at work all around us, we have incredible hope.

During World War II, there was a decisive day that determined the outcome of the war. It was D-Day, June 5, 1944. On D-Day, the Allied forces landed on the beaches of Normandy, and the invasion of Nazi territory began. Both Rommel on the Nazi side and Eisenhower on the Allied side were well aware that whichever side prevailed on that day would be the eventual victor. Everyone everywhere knew that this battle would determine the outcome of World War II.

We now know that on D-Day the beachhead was established and the Allied forces prevailed. On that day, the Allies assured their eventual triumph by breaking the power of the Nazis. Yet there would be months and months of suffering still ahead. Hundreds of thousands of people would shed their blood. Actually, more men and women would die on the battlefield *after* D-Day than before D-Day. But there was good news on D-Day—the outcome of the war was no longer in question. Eisenhower knew it, and Rommel knew it.

So certain was the outcome of the war that Rommel tried to cut the losses of Germany by attempting an assassination of Hitler and moving towards an early peace. Rommel failed, and Germany moved on to inexorable destruction. But the point is that D-Day assured the world that V-Day (the day when the enemy finally surrendered) would one day come.

What Eastern Orthodox theology teaches is that all of nature is in a period that can be likened to that which stood between D-Day and V-Day. Through the cross and resurrection, God has already established a beachhead in history and has given us the assurance that His light and His legions ultimately will win. The animals have suffered since D-Day. The rest of nature has also suffered. And humanity itself has suffered most of all. But all *shall* be delivered. All *will* be "saved." There *will* be an end at which time Satan will surrender, and the armies he commanded will be bound. A day is coming when, not only the human race, but all of creation will be delivered from its suffering. On that day, the sufferings of animals will end, and the rest of nature will rediscover the peace and joy that God willed for them when He created them.

WHAT THE THINKERS ARE THINKING

What Christian Theologians Have to Say

I suppose that I was about seven years old when I popped the question: "Do animals go to heaven when they die?"

My family never had a dog, but our next door neighbors did. And I got to play with her. She was one of those "special" dogs you can get from the S.P.C.A. She was brown and curly, and whenever she saw me, she would dance and jump around. She made me feel more special than anyone else did.

Pretty (that was her name) had one very bad habit. She loved to chase cars, and that was her undoing. The Sunday after she was killed, I wanted my Sunday school teacher to tell me whether I would ever see Pretty again.

He didn't know!

But he's not the only one. It is amazing how little the theologians and biblical scholars know about animals. I suppose I could forgive them if they had not paid much attention to inanimate nature. I even could understand if they did not have anything to say about flowers and other plants. But not to have anything to say about animals, especially those animals who become our close friends, raises all kinds of questions about whether they know what is really important. Certainly, as a seven-year-old boy, I felt they had left an important question unanswered.

I want you to go with me as I explore and discuss what the Bible has to say about nature. And I want you to do some careful thinking about what the great theologians of the Christian faith have to tell us about what the Bible says. I want to start by focusing on what they have said about those creatures of God that are nearest and dearest to us—the animals.

STARTING WITH FRANCIS

I think that the most profound and thorough insight about animals and their place in God's creation comes from one who might be called the greatest saint of the church since New Testament days—St. Francis of Assisi. Most people are familiar with St. Francis because of the many St. Francis statues that we see in gardens and on lawns. These statues serve to remind us of the special relationship Francis had with animals. His preaching to the birds is the most common image of this medieval Italian saint, and the Roman Catholic order he founded works hard to perpetuate Francis's deep spiritual affinity for all of nature.

To Francis, the animals were sacramental. They were, to him, a special means of grace. He believed that, through the animals, we could experience something of Christ. It was his conviction that every encounter with animals, if entered into with true spiritual sensitivity, could be an encounter with the Lord. Perhaps at the core of his teaching was the belief that when Jesus told His disciples that whatever they did to the "least of these My brethren" they would be doing to Him (Matthew 25:40), Jesus meant the animals to be included among "the least." There can be no doubt Francis sensed a spiritual kinship with animals and believed that through them God was trying to reach us and bless us. To Francis, animals were "brothers and sisters."

We must recognize that even though Francis affirmed the spiritual significance that animals have for us, he should not be identified with pantheism (the philosophy that declares God and nature are one and the same). For Francis, God was always a transcendental "totally other" figure who existed before the world was created and who was the Creator of the world. But Francis believed that even though our God totally transcends nature, He still expresses Himself in and through all the things He has created, especially in and through all of His living creatures. If Francis were with us, He would quote the Scriptures which say:

> For since the creation of the world His invisible attributes are clearly seen, being understood by the things

that are made, even his eternal power and Godhead, so that they are without excuse. (Romans 1:20)

To illustrate what Francis was talking about, allow me to refer to the view Lutherans hold about the sacrament of Holy Communion. According to the Lutherans, transubstantiation does not occur. (Transubstantiation is the doctrine that in the Mass the bread and wine are miraculously transformed into the body and blood of Christ.) They believe that in Holy Communion the bread remains bread and the wine remains wine. But Lutherans do believe that there comes *into* the bread and *into* the wine a real presence of Christ. While the elements do not become the flesh and blood of Jesus, Lutherans believe Jesus does become a real presence in them—so when the communicants eat the bread and drink from the cup, they simultaneously receive the presence of Christ into their lives.

In a similar way, Francis believed the animals become hosts for the real presence of Christ. While believing that Jesus remained distinct from the animals, Francis nevertheless believed that Jesus spoke through the animals to us, thus providing us with special opportunities for encounters with God.

The twentieth-century Jewish philosopher, Martin Buber, picked up on this Franciscan theme when he wrote about how we should relate to animals. Buber, too, believed God could be found in our encounters with animals. According to Buber, whether or not we feel God in nature and in animals depends on the way we relate to God, to others, and to the rest of God's creations. One way is to have an "I-It" relationship, and the other is to have an "I-Thou" relationship.[1]

As persons, we can choose to relate to animals as though they were nothing more than "things" or "its."

We can treat them as being devoid of any spiritual presence. We can decide to use them rather than love them. And, if we merely use them, we will probably relate to them as though they were objects.

Animals, according to Buber, can be treated as creatures with no essential personalities. They can be regarded as nothing more than biological organisms without any capacity for the kind of consciousness that is a prerequisite for a personal relationship. On the other hand, Buber contends that it is possible to experience a mystical kind of oneness with animals. We can have an "I-Thou" relationship with them.

The "I-Thou" is possible outside of human relationships, and those who are rightly disposed toward animals can encounter something far more than flesh and blood. It is possible, Buber tells us, to "enter into" the personality of an animal and to connect with something very spiritual in these special creatures of God. It is possible to have communion with the animals and in that communion to experience something of the "Eternal Thou." Buber contends it is possible for something to happen in relationships with animals that can put one in touch with God.

Buber talks about the relationship he had with his cat in terms that have the feel of St. Francis. Buber talks about looking deeply into his cat's eyes, and he describes those moments in which he feels like he is "entering into" the cat and experiences something of the cat's subjectivity. In what he would call an "I-Thou" encounter, Buber claims he is able to take on the cat's consciousness in some strange and mysterious way. Even as God is able to enter into each of us and get that inner feeling for life we have, so it is that in the "I-Thou" with his cat, Buber claims to be able to gain the consciousness and feelings his cat has as she gazes out upon her world.

St. Francis would have understood what Buber is trying to say to us. St. Francis knew of the awesome wonder that can come upon any person who is willing to lovingly receive what comes from an animal and what is available when that animal lovingly surrenders to the person in return. The ecstatic oneness of the "I-Thou" is very much what St. Francis experienced when he encountered animals. And for St. Francis, such moments of sacred oneness with God while experiencing a loving relationship with animals were a common everyday experience.

Those who walked through life with St. Francis talked of his special relationship with animals. There are the accounts of sheep looking up from their feeding when St. Francis came near them and running to him to receive a blessing. St. Bonaventure, who knew Francis, contends that on such occasions, Francis would invite the sheep to sing praises to God. Francis would first show his love for the sheep. Then he would invite the sheep to "bah" to the glory of God.

What was it about Francis that led the sheep to stop their grazing and seek a blessing from a strange man dressed in burlap?

How was it possible for a mere mortal to overcome the limits of his own creatureliness and enter into the subjectivity of dumb animals?

What powers from God did this man possess, and is it possible for us to learn to exercise such powers in our day and age?

It was not only with the animals that Francis had such glorious empathy and communion. According to the reports of those who lived with him, Francis was even able to commune with insects. This man, who was so close to

Jesus that he, like Paul, bore the bleeding wounds of the crucifixion on his body, also had a closeness to all the creatures his Jesus had created—even insects.

According to legend there was one cricket which supposedly drew the attention of Francis one night as he tried to sleep. Instead of being irritated by this lowly insect and hushing it in one way or another, Francis invited the cricket to join him in prayer. Not only did Francis teach the cricket to make music for the Lord's pleasure, but Francis invited the cricket to return each day at the same time to share a prayer time with him. And St. Bonaventure tells us the cricket did just that.

Were these the made-up stories of enamored followers, or are these true historical accounts of what really happened?

Are we to accept these seemingly impossible events as empirical truth, or are we to regard them as apocryphal stories meant to teach us some of the values that St. Francis wanted us to learn?

Did Jesus give to Francis the power to do some things even Jesus Himself did not do, thus fulfilling His prophecy?

> Most assuredly, I say to you, he who believes in Me, the works that I do he will do also; and greater works than these he will do, because I go to My Father. (John 14:12)

I tend to believe these tales of wonder even though they violate the commonly accepted scientific canons of what can be real. I am ready to accept the testimony of those whose firsthand experiences left them convinced that St. Francis could talk to the birds and share something profound with all the rest of God's creation.

I suppose you could call me an evangelical Protestant Franciscan because I believe in what St. Francis taught. I believe he was a man with such a close relationship to Jesus that he became like Jesus as he met the animals and enjoyed being part of a family that stretched beyond the limited circle of relatives that make up the human race.

One of the stories which is usually included in the many accounts written about the life of St. Francis is the story of how he saved a wolf hated by the people of Assisi.

The town in which St. Francis lived consisted of farmers and shepherds. Most of them were not rich and could ill afford to lose what little they had. Thus, the shepherds of Assisi were more than angry when their herds became the target of a killer wolf who seemed to have an insatiable appetite.

Night after night, herds were raided, and morning after morning, the shepherds returned to their grazing field to find the carcasses of the latest victims. When they could put up with this menace no longer, they came together and decided that as a group they would hunt down and kill the terrible wolf and thus be freed from the threat to their livelihood.

When Francis heard the news he rushed to talk with the angry shepherds. He pleaded with the men and finally struck a bargain with them. He asked them to let him go out and find the wolf and try to deal with the problem without killing the animal. If Francis failed, then he would support the shepherds' plan to kill the wolf. Out of respect for this holy man, the shepherds of Assisi agreed and allowed Francis to have first crack at this wild and dangerous wolf.

St. Francis disappeared into the hills, and when he returned a few days later, there—to the surprise of everyone—was the wolf at his side. The animal was tame and gentle. Francis had loved the animal into being a pet. With his caring empathy, he had made the wolf into a friend, or as he would say, "a brother." And until the wolf died, he lived among the people of Assisi as their friend too.

I like this story about St. Francis because I believe that it very much illustrates a way in which we can carry out our God-ordained rule as His agents for the restoration of nature. In relating to the wolf with a love that flowed from his relationship with Christ, Francis was able to tame a wild creature and make it part of a human community. With a love like the love expressed in Jesus, Francis was able to have the kind of "I-Thou" relationship with the wolf that could rescue the animal from its fallen state of violence. Francis had made it a part of his Christian calling to bring the wolf into what the Bible calls *shalom*, which is that peaceful kingdom where God's will and love are lived out in all relationships. The *shalom* of God is that kingdom in which men and women have redemptive and restorative friendships with each other and where people are also willing to extend that friendship to the nonhuman world in which they live.

A MISSING LINK IN METHODIST THEOLOGY

John Wesley, the founder of Methodism, was another Christian who had a deep spiritual burden for animals. It was Wesley's conviction that animals were sadly and unwittingly caught up in the consequences of the fall of the human race. The curse which fell upon Adam and Eve because of their primal disobedience to God in the Garden of Eden was, according to Wesley, a curse that brought suffering to the animal kingdom. What happened to us as a result of the Fall happened also to them.

Wesley was saddened that innocent creatures suffered because of the evil committed by Adam and Eve. Furthermore, he sensed an injustice in all of this. "Why should the animals be subjected to suffering and violence when they have committed no sin?" he asked. Why should they go through pain and live out their lives in constant fear because of sin that was not their own?

It was Wesley's personal belief that someday God in His justice must provide some kind of salvation for the animals. He suggested God might even have to compensate the animals for their undue sufferings by allowing them to share in eternal life and heaven. Wesley asked:

> But will "the creature," will even the brute creature, always remain in this deplorable condition? God forbid that we should affirm this; yea, or even entertain such a thought![2]

He went on to declare:

> He seeth "the earnest expectation" wherewith the whole animated creation "waiteth for" that final "manifestation of the sons of God"; in which "they themselves also shall be delivered" (not by annihilation; annihilation is not deliverance) "from the" present bondage of corruption, into "a *measure* of" the glorious liberty of the children of God.[3]

Further Wesley preached:

> They will be restored, not only to that measure of understanding which they had in paradise, but to a degree of it as much higher than that, as the understanding of an

elephant is beyond that of a worm. And whatever affections they had in the garden of God, will be restored with vast increase. . . . They will be delivered from all irregular appetites, from all unruly passions, from every disposition that is either evil in itself, or has any tendency to evil. No rage will be found in any creature, no fierceness, no cruelty, or thirst for blood.[4]

Without question, Wesley believed that when Jesus returns and creates the new heaven and the new earth, the animals will live in a perfect environment which will be to them "one perennial spring." In this future paradise, Wesley believed God "will make large amends to them for all they suffer while under their present bondage." If Wesley had been my Sunday school teacher when I was seven years old, he would have told me that dogs like my neighbor's dog, Pretty, would be given a place in the kingdom of God. Wesley's gospel was not only filled with hope for people, but for the animals too.

HEAVEN FOR ANIMALS

Modern-day evangelicals have made C. S. Lewis into a patron saint. This Oxford don has provided the evangelical community with some of its best literature and apologetics. Books by Lewis are a standard part of any evangelical scholar's library. Term papers by students at Christian colleges are sprinkled with quotes from books like *Mere Christianity* and *The Problem of Pain*. But most evangelicals would be surprised to find that their intellectual hero espoused a doctrine they might consider heretical—the resurrection of animals.

According to Lewis, animals can be so much a part of our lives they become part of who we are. As such, our resurrection must encompass their resurrection too. When we "humanize" animals by making them our pets, they are *in* us. They share in our personhood. They enter into the spiritual depths of our being. Accordingly, Lewis believed our resurrection would be less than it ought to be if our animals did not share it with us. Their future is tied up with the people who love them. Their only resurrection is in relationship with those who have made them part of their lives. We "save" animals, Lewis claimed, by training them and incorporating them into our own destiny. Lewis wrote:

> The beasts are to be understood only in their relation to man and, through man, to God. . . . Now it will be seen that, in so far as the tame animal has a real self or personality, it owes this almost entirely to its master. . . . If a good sheepdog seems "almost human" that is because a good shepherd has made it so.[5]

Animals are "in" us in a way Lewis claimed is analogous to the way we are "in" Christ. Thus even as our eternal life is "in Him," so the resurrection of the animals is tied up with our resurrection. In his famous book *The Problem of Pain*, Lewis wrote the following:

> I am now going to suggest . . . that there may be a sense, corresponding, though not identical, with these, in which those beasts that attain a real self are in their masters. That is to say, you must not think of a beast by itself, and call that a personality and then inquire whether God will raise and bless that. You must take the whole context in which the beast acquires its self-hood—namely "The-goodman-and-the-goodwife-ruling-their-children-and-their-beasts-in-the-good-homestead."

. . . And in this way it seems to me possible that certain animals may have an immortality, not in themselves, but in the immortality of their masters.[6]

Note that Lewis said "possible." His views were based on intellectual speculation and inference. There is no biblical support for this theology.

LIBERATION THEOLOGIANS GET INTO THE ACT

Whether mainline Christians, fundamentalists, evangelicals, and charismatics like it or not, liberation theology has become very much a part of theological studies these days. Christians everywhere, even when they bitterly oppose the use of violence advocated by some liberation theologians or abhor the Marxist-Leninist implications in much of what they hear, still agree with the basic theme of liberation theology: Christ has come into the world to set all of creation free from the oppression of sin and the power of Satan. Most of them are ready to agree this oppression is not only evident in the personal lives of people, but also in political structures and in economic institutions.

As of late, there is much evidence that liberation theologies are beginning to be applied to environmental concerns and to the animal rights movement. More and more, there are declarations in sermons and in books that the liberating God is also at work in the world delivering His enslaved creation from the hands of those who have abused it through the misuse of power. More specifically, the animal rights people who operate out of a Christian theological base have found in liberation theology some needed arguments to make their case to the church.

This new version of liberation theology regards the work of the Messiah to be: first, the deliverance of humanity from sin and death; second, the deliverance of oppressed people into the freedom and well-being that God the Father intends for all people; and third, the deliverance of all of creation from those oppressive powers that would exploit and destroy it in the name of profits. God, they claim, is a God of love who calls us to live in harmony with nature and therefore to stand against those who would disregard environmental concerns in their lust for wealth and in their ambition to dominate.

Their Jesus is the liberator who will end the tyranny of the power-hungry, greedy, evil landlords who have turned Eden into a desert in their quest to satisfy their appetite for things. Those who have exploited the environment are viewed as the merchants described in the book of Revelation who have identified with the Antichrist. The havoc they create was envisioned by the apostle John:

> Standing at a distance for fear of her torment, saying, "Alas, alas, that great city Babylon, that mighty city! For in one hour your judgement has come." And the merchants of the earth will weep and mourn over her, for no one buys their merchandise any more. (Revelation 18:10–11)

The "peaceable kingdom" that the theologically sensitized advocates of animal liberation believe the Messiah will bring in at His second coming will be one in which the oppression of animals will end. On that great day, even the animals themselves will live in harmony with each other, and the violence which has characterized the jungle that replaced the Garden will be no more.

Disciples of Christ, according to this theology of liberation, should be committed to the ministry which Christ will complete at His return. They should declare the deliverance of humans from sin, work for a just society wherein all forms of oppression will end, and be committed to liberating an exploited animal kingdom from its suffering.

With so many species already hunted to extinction and so many others being highly endangered, it is time for evangelical Christians to become partners with the Messiah of history in the deliverance of the threatened creation.

6

*G*OD IN THE CHICKEN COOP

The Sufferings of Animals

*S*pinning theories about the ultimate fate of animals has its place, particularly for those of us who have become especially fond of our pets. But as we Christians think about nature, there are concerns with what is happening to nature—and specifically to animals—right now. We should ask ourselves what biblical principles should guide us in the way we treat animals. And we should ask ourselves what God has to say about the *unnecessary* suffering we bring into their lives.

Once when I was trying to get a discussion going with some of my students, I asked the simple question, "Does God love chickens?"

I know that the question seems silly—but think again. *Does* God love chickens?

Does the God who gave life to chickens and who sustains them by His grace really care about them?

Does the One who sees and cares for every sparrow that falls (Matthew 10:29–31) feel for those common, two-legged creatures?

Does He feel their pain?

Does He experience the subjective side of these simple barnyard animals?

If you can say yes to such questions, then consider what Patrick Goldring tells us in his book *The Broiler House Society* about how chickens are raised and slaughtered for market:

> Barely visible in a dim red light are several thousand chickens crowded wing to wing and jostling around the food hoppers and water bowls spaced at intervals down the gloomy length of the shed. There is underfloor electric heating. Food and water are provided automatically. The ventilator extracts some of the smell, disinfectant is sprayed regularly, and the wood shavings on the floor are turned over occasionally to cover the droppings. Chicks come here from hatcheries one day after they are hatched and spend their entire lives—a precisely calculated sixty days—inside the broiler house. Until the day they die, they never see the sun, never feel the wind or the rain, never set foot on honest earth.[1]

I don't know how you feel, but I find it hard to believe that God, who Jesus says is concerned about every sparrow, is indifferent to all of this.

When God creates, He creates for "good" (Genesis 1). God instills a potential for a "good life" in all of His creatures, and those chickens never realize that potential. There is reason to believe that when God creates, He creates creatures whose satisfactions and sufferings become His own.

I believe the sufferings of these chickens are sufferings He feels.

I believe when He put creatures on this planet, He willed His glory to be expressed in their lives. But this kind of living only testifies to the presence of demonic agony in the world.

I believe when God created chickens, He wanted them to reflect His joy and peace. But their cries of pain contradict all of that. If you think the suffering of chickens is a contradiction to the will of God, then their dying will disturb you even more.

They are shackled by their legs to conveyor belts and hung with their heads down so the blood can be concentrated in their heads and easily drained from their bodies when their throats are cut. Still not dead, they are carried through a "bleeding tunnel" and then lowered into a scalding tank. Two out of three of them go into the tank alive.

Those who argue that (as unfortunate as this painful treatment of chickens might be) it is necessary to provide the food that we need, are ignoring the facts. We overproduce chickens. We have to advertise in order to stimulate the overconsumption that keeps the chicken economy going. And even if we did need the mass slaughtering of chickens in order to provide us with food, there have to be more humane ways of doing it.

Animals seem so innocent and undeserving of the pain that usually accompanies their living and dying. Why do they have to suffer so much? Why do they have to endure so much pain? Some theologians, like the medieval Roman Catholic theologian Thomas Aquinas, have tried to make the animals themselves responsible.

St. Thomas Aquinas believed animals sinned and thus fell from grace before there ever was an Adam and Eve. Accordingly, Aquinas suggested that the suffering of animals is their just due.

Before Aquinas, St. Augustine gave another explanation. Augustine taught that "the fall" of animals was somehow linked to the fall of Satan (Ezekiel 28:13–19). When Satan rebelled against God and was cast out of heaven, argued Augustine, he not only took a third of the heavenly hosts with him, but he also brought the animal kingdom into his camp of destruction and suffering.

Generally, contemporary Christian scholars believe the plight of animals is somehow connected with the fall of humankind in the Garden of Eden. In ways these scholars find difficult to explain, there is supposedly some spiritual link between human beings and the rest of nature. The destiny of animals, consequently, is inexorably tied up with the destiny of the children of the human race. Most theologians claim the sin of Adam and Eve corrupted nature, and humanity's mystical tie with nature has dire consequences for the animals. Accordingly, the sufferings and pain animals must endure in their struggles for existence come from a curse that was brought upon them through no fault of their own.

But for most of us, such theologies seem inadequate and unsatisfactory. John Hick, a theologian who has given a great deal of thought to all of this, speaks for many of us when he says, "The suffering of animals constitutes one of the most baffling aspects of the 'problem of evil.' "[2]

Whatever animals may have suffered as the result of the first sin in the Garden, I think most of us would agree there is little doubt the sin of the human race in today's world is what really lies behind most of the pain and death animals must now endure. It is our perversity, not theirs, that creates most of their pain. Irresponsible stewardship of God's creation and our greedy exploitation of natural resources have wrought the unbelievable suffering that seems evident everywhere in the animal kingdom.

THE SUFFERINGS WE BRING TO ANIMALS

Who among us has witnessed the television shots of sea gulls, ducks, and other birds covered with black gook from oil spills and has not shuddered with the awareness of what our sinful carelessness has brought upon the innocent? We hear that the captain of the tanker was drunk before running his ship against some rocks. Then we learn that the oil company, trying to maximize profits, assumed a reckless attitude so far as precautions were concerned. But amid all the accusations and counteraccusations, we sense that the sinful nature of people is behind the plight of these creatures.

As we watch pathetic birds trying to squirm away from the caring helpers attempting to wipe away the black ooze covering their bodies, we have ample testimony to our race's inhumane indifference to God's creation. We sense, in the midst of such scenes, that human lust for wealth and power lies behind the suffering these unfortunate creatures must endure. The painful sight of dying birds flapping their wings to no avail is all we need to recognize that behind this ecological disaster is something for which human beings must bear the guilt.

When the Greenpeace people flash before us the videos of baby seals being clubbed to death, we cringe a bit but try to tell ourselves it is a necessary evil. We tell ourselves that in the grand scheme of things the killing of baby seals isn't very important. We may even make jokes about the bumper stickers that try to create an awareness of the slaughter. But all the time, we know these innocent animals lose their lives, not to meet a need, but to gratify a selfish want.

People really do not *need* the fur coats this suffering and death necessitates. Other materials can provide the fabric for coats that would be just as attractive and keep us just as warm.

We are told this slaughtering of baby seals is a necessary evil for some people to make a living. But even that is not a sufficient excuse. We know that other ways could be devised for these people to support their families.

Causing unnecessary pain in the animal kingdom is sin. People lose something of their humanity when they destroy life in order to provide items of luxury for the affluent. They give up something precious in their souls when they club baby seals into unconsciousness in order to get pelts that really are not needed.

It was different when seals were killed in order to provide meat for a hungry tribe or to provide warm coats to protect people against the arctic cold. Since Eden, it has been justifiable to kill a lower species to provide a means for survival for a higher species. We must accept this as a regrettable reality that goes with living in our fallen world.

But that is not what is going on here. We see before us in the slaughtering of baby seals the promotion of death in order to serve the life-styles of the rich. We see a completely unnecessary practice that brings pain and death to creatures God loves.

MEDICAL TESTING ON ANIMALS

Romans 8:19–21 tells us that the Holy Spirit sensitizes us to the agonies of animals. This passage also tells us that when the Holy Spirit is in us and becomes a motivating force in our lives, He drives us to work to alleviate these agonies.

One of the ways Christians can demonstrate their readiness to be led by the Holy Spirit is by making a commitment to the animal rights movement. Please do not let the behavior of extremists in this movement keep you out. Most good movements, even the church, attract their share of crazies. You should be involved. Working to end the unnecessary sufferings of animals has been designated in this passage in Romans as a calling of God and a duty of those of us who are heirs to Pentecost.

Personally, I see the crusade to end the unnecessary sufferings of animals as a vital part of my Christian faith. I differ with some of those in the movement in that I believe some of the suffering which we inflict on the animal kingdom can be legitimate and actually does serve some good purposes.

For instance, I believe using animals in certain medical experiments is a necessary evil that can be rationally justified. Ethicists easily can make the case that, in order to ensure the life and well-being of humans, it is sometimes necessary to sacrifice the lives of animals. But what makes me willing to lend my limited support to the animal rights movement is my commitment to abolishing the *unnecessary* torturing and killing of animals. And there is more of that going on than most Christians suspect.

Recently, the famous actor Jimmy Stewart, testifying before a special committee of the U.S. Congress, drew attention to the unnecessary and unwarranted torturing of animals that goes on in the cosmetic industry. He described how rabbits were forced to go through excruciating suffering for no other reason than to determine how mascara would affect their eyes. Rabbits, he explained, were held tightly by the neck in special devices as cosmetics were applied to their faces. The only movement these devices allowed was the squirming of the lower parts of their bodies. In many cases, the eyes of the rabbits became infected by the mascara, and their little bodies twisted and turned in pain. Jimmy Stewart, his voice choked with sorrow, told the congressional hearing how he watched some of the rabbits break their backs and die because of the extreme convulsions brought on by pain. He said, "It is wrong for animals to have to endure such suffering in order to provide makeup for women."

I agree with him. How many chimpanzees and monkeys have been tortured and abused, not for a high and lofty purpose like seeking a cure for cancer or AIDS, but to provide insensitive scientists with the opportunity to carry out unnecessary experiments or to test some frivolous product? How many small animals have been jabbed with needles and subjected to slow and painful deaths, not in a noble medical effort to find a cure for something like Lyme disease, but to find out which product makes for curlier hair? The record is clear. We are making animals endure incredible pain without sufficient justification. I cannot believe Jesus is pleased with all of this. Animals should be used for *necessary* medical experiments but never for the development of beauty aids and toiletries. And when animal testing is warranted, every effort should be made to minimize the pain the animals have to endure.

At one leading Ivy League university, nearly a million dollars a year was spent over a period of five years doing "brain-bashing" experiments on baboons. The heads of these animals were cemented into metal helmets and then connected to a specially designed hydraulic device. This device was designed to regularly smash the heads of the baboons against the helmets with a force of up to 1,000g's (15g's is sufficient to kill a human being). All of this was to simulate the kinds of head injuries people experience in boxing matches, football games, and automobile accidents. There is ample evidence to show there was an absence of adequate anesthesia during these experiments. These suffering creatures endured horrible torture that easily could have been prevented.[3]

One of the most significant arguments of the animal rights people is that a good number of the tests being conducted on animals are completely unnecessary.

A published report states that Avon Products, Inc., a company which once killed almost twenty-four thousand animals a year in its experiments, has changed its ways. It has switched to using a new procedure to determine whether or not its products irritate the skin or the eyes. In this new experiment, known as the Eytex method, a vegetable protein is used to imitate the cornea's reaction to foreign matter. Thus, it has become unnecessary to test cosmetics on the eyes of animals.[4]

In another company, Ropek Industries of Irvine, California, created a new formula using pumpkin rind which makes it possible to mimic the reaction of human skin to foreign substances.[5]

We now find that computer models can predict what reactions humans will have to various drugs so that much testing becomes unnecessary. Computers in many instances can calculate human reactions to injuries better than animal testing methods.

HUNTING—A CHRISTIAN PERSPECTIVE

In dealing with the unnecessary and unwarranted sufferings of animals, it is important to once again pick up our discussion of hunting. Every year, tens of thousands of wounded deer limp off into the woods to suffer and die. Every year there are significant numbers of animals whose lives end in great pain.

I could never figure out how hunters justify making a sport out of hunting. To kill animals with regret because the meat is needed for food may be understandable and necessary. To kill animals to eliminate a threat of attack and death may, at times, be brave. To kill some deer to cut the size of the herd to a point where starvation from a limited food supply is prevented may even be noble. But to make killing into a sport is quite another thing. To make killing *fun* is inhumane. Or, to put it more directly, I believe that to kill *for the fun of it* is a sin against God.

I have heard the case for hunting. I have listened to the explanations of how it fosters male bonding and builds great relationships between father and son. But as I listen, I am always asking myself whether it ever occurs to these defenders of a sport based on killing that there might be a more humane way of gaining these kinds of blessings? I have to ask myself whether hunters ever consider what might be happening to themselves and their sons in the context of making a sport of tracking down animals and then killing them. Do they ever ask, "Is this what Jesus would do?"

One man who pushed me on this subject contended strongly that hunting was part of what made him a man. He told me he was going to make sure his son had a chance to become the same kind of man. But I wondered if he had considered just what kind of man he had become and what kind of man his son would become because of hunting. Has the sport of hunting made either of them more compassionate and sensitive? Has hunting stirred in either of them the kindness and gentleness which the Scriptures tell us are fruits of the Spirit?

The psalmist David, who was himself a hunter, recognized that God has compassion for all animals in His creation. He writes in Psalm 145:9, "The LORD is good to all, / And His tender mercies are over all His works."

David recognized that God empathizes with animals, that He subjectively entered into their pain. We also know that David was, in accord with what is said in Scripture, "a man after God's own heart." As David hunted for food, something of God's sorrow about a world in which killing is a part of living must have been in his heart too.

The compassion God has for His animals is graphically depicted in His response to the sin of Nineveh. In the famous story of Jonah and the whale, the Lord commands His servant Jonah to go to the wicked city of Nineveh and warn the people who live there that unless they repent, they and their city will be destroyed. God wants to save Nineveh from destruction, not only because He loves the sinful people who live there but also because He loves the animals that make Nineveh their home (Jonah 4:6–11). Apparently, God feels pangs of mercy toward creatures who have to suffer for no other crime than having been caught up in the affairs of sinful people.

Killing animals may, at times, prove necessary. The hunter who brings home food for his or her family may be doing a relatively good thing. The Scriptures say nothing that prohibits the eating of meat. Actually, the Bible warns against those who would make vegetarianism some kind of religious law or a requisite for spirituality. But I am convinced the kind of character and loving sensitivity the Lord seeks to build in us is not really encouraged by hunting. Furthermore, I contend that struggling to curtail hunting and, in so doing, helping to diminish the groanings and the moanings of nature is what Romans 8:19–23 requires of us. Theology, in the end, must get down to such practical things.

It is the responsibility of every parent to build into every child the kind of thinking and feeling that was in Christ Jesus (Philippians 2:1). And in 1 Corinthians 9:9, we are told by the apostle Paul that our Lord is full of compassion toward all of His creation. Jesus holds a place in His heart for animals. He made friends with them, and they were His companions in His wilderness experience (Mark 1:13). If that hunter father who argued with me wanted to make his son like Jesus, might he not have to change his attitude about hunting?

7

PARADISE LOST

Sin and Salvation in Creation

Nature feels things even when people do not sense what is going on. Certainly that was true the day that Jesus died. The hills outside Jerusalem responded to His crucifixion by trembling. As Christ hung on the cross, the skies darkened and thunder shook the city (Luke 23:44–45). When the Lord surrendered to death on Good Friday, there was an angry response from all of creation:

> And behold, the veil of the temple was torn in two from top to bottom; and the earth quaked, and the rocks were split. (Matthew 27:51)

So awesome were the effects of Christ's death upon nature, so violently did the earth react, that those who stood by and watched were struck with fear, wonder, and even grudging belief:

> Now when the centurion and those with him, who were guarding Jesus, saw the earthquake and the things that had happened, they feared greatly, saying, "Truly this was the Son of God!" (Matthew 27:54)

Nature understood what most of those who were in and around Jerusalem did not seem able to grasp.

It is hard for us rational children of the Enlightenment to believe that anything lower than the animals has any kind of responsive feelings. Most people will give me some grace when I claim that animals have feelings and that God, in His infinite knowledge of all things, is able to empathize with them when they suffer. But when I refer to plants and soil as having feelings, I am stretching folks way beyond what their imaginations can readily handle. But nature does have some kind of capacity to "feel," even if its feelings are totally other than anything we can understand.

The Bible is clear that there was something in the wind and in the waves that could respond to the commands of Jesus. In the famous biblical account of our Lord's stilling the troubled seas in the midst of a storm, Jesus spoke to the elements of nature, and they obeyed Him. And the words that He used in appealing to the winds and waves were most significant: He said, "Peace, be still." In His own words, He pleaded with the winds and the waves to surrender to the *shalom* of His Father. (The peace of God—*shalom*—is that stillness that reflects the harmonious equilibrium that pervades the world when His will is done and when all things are what God meant them to be.)

The disciples recognized that something more than a magical display of power had been exercised before their eyes. They whispered to one another that even the winds and the waves obeyed Him:

Now when He got into a boat, His disciples followed
Him. And suddenly a great tempest arose on the sea,
so that the boat was covered with the waves. But He
was asleep. Then His disciples came to Him and
awoke Him, saying, "Lord, save us! We are perishing!"
But He said to them, "Why are you fearful, O you of
little faith?" Then He arose and rebuked the winds
and the sea. And there was a great calm. And the men
marveled, saying, "Who can this be, that even the
winds and the sea obey Him?" (Matthew 8:23–27)

There are all kinds of references to the trees responding in joy to the glory of God (Isaiah 55:12) and the
mountains giving forth praise (Isaiah 49:13, 55:12). Generally, we claim that such passages of Scripture are poetic and not to be taken literally. But then again, we may
be wrong.

Certainly the Christian mystics sensed a spiritual empathy with nature. St. Francis, in his famous prayer *Can-
ticle of the Sun*, calls the sun and the moon his brother
and sister and lets us know that he has a kind of personal relationship with them:

Canticle of the Sun

O most high, almighty, good Lord God, to thee belong
praise, glory, honor, and all blessing.

Praised be my Lord God with all his creatures and especially our brother the sun, who brings us the day
and who brings us the light; fair is he and shines with
a very great splendor: O Lord, he signifies to us Thee.

Praised be my Lord for our sister the moon, and for
the stars, the which he hath set clear and lovely in the
heavens.

Praised be my Lord for our brother the wind, and for the air and cloud, calms and all weather by the which thou upholdest life in all creatures.

Praised be my Lord for our sister water, who is very serviceable unto us and humble and precious and clean.

Praised be my Lord for our brother fire, through which thou givest us light in the darkness; and he is bright and pleasant and very mighty and strong.

Praised be my Lord for our mother the earth, the which doth sustain us and keep us, and bringeth forth divers fruits and flowers of many colors, and grass.

Praised be my Lord for all those who pardon one another for his love's sake, and who endure weakness and tribulation; blessed are they who peaceably shall endure, for thou, O most Highest, shalt give them a crown.

Praise ye and bless the Lord and give thanks unto him and serve him with great humility.

I realize that I am treading on dangerous ground when I talk about such empathy with the elements of creation and with plants and trees. In all of this there is something dangerously close to the ravings of those New Age crazies who talk of their special communion with nature. And yet perhaps in what they say, as in most heresies, there is a grain of truth. Might it be that the New Age people, with their personalization of nature, have taken some element of God's truth and twisted and distorted it to serve demonic purposes? Those who are experts on heresies readily point out that most heresies are created out of neglected Christian truths which are picked up and exaggerated in ways that lead people away from the truth of God.

In all that I am saying here, I am deliberately avoiding any suggestion of pantheism. Nature is not divine.

God is "totally other" than nature. I do not want to be misconstrued in this. Only human beings were created by God to have souls (Genesis 2:7). But I am saying that there is something volitional and spontaneous about nature that is capable of reaching out to God. There is something inherent in creation that is capable of glorifying and worshiping God. "The heavens declare the glory of God; / And the firmament shows His handiwork" (Psalm 19:1).

Modern science lends some validity to such a theology of nature. For instance, the "feelings" of flowers have been examined by studies on how they respond to human emotions. When in close proximity to harsh words and mean attitudes, flowers have been observed to wilt. It is as though the hurts we humans inflict on one another are felt by the flowers so that they experience hurt too.

On the other hand, when flowers are surrounded by kind and loving messages between nearby people, they tend to display an unusual capacity to blossom. In some experiments, responses have been observed in flowers when certain people speak directly to them. Once again, kind and gentle words seem to elicit blooms, while harsh and mean words seem to cause withering and drooping. It is as though the plants blossom and shine in the context of *shalom*, and that the more the *shalom* of God is shown to them, the more gloriously they respond. I am suggesting that, just as the first Adam's sin permeated nature and fostered violence and death, so the righteous *shalom* of the second Adam, as expressed through those who are willing to be channels of it, can permeate nature, bring healing to it, and restore something of its former glory.

FINDING SPIRITUAL GROUND IN SCIENCE

In making the case for the capacity of nature to respond to those who, like St. Francis, are endowed with the Spirit of Christ, I find some help in Heisenberg's Theory of Indeterminacy. According to those who understand this rather involved theory of quantum physics, even the world of molecules and atoms may not be quite as mechanical as we have previously thought. Scientists are now telling us that there may be a volitional quality to atoms. Those who think that everything in the physical universe is governed by natural laws may be in for quite a jolt when confronted with some of the implications of Werner Heisenberg's discovery.

What Heisenberg tells us is that there are no known physical forces that determine the movements of electrons around the nucleus of an atom. Furthermore, electrons from time to time change directions. Their orbits around the atom's nucleus can be altered, and there is apparently no way to explain why these electrons behave as they do. The electrons just seem to have a will of their own. They appear to exhibit a kind of spontaneous free choice.

I remember my surprise when I asked Enos Witmer, a physicist at the University of Pennsylvania, why he thought that electrons changed the directions of their orbits from time to time and why they behaved in a somewhat erratic fashion. He responded, with a whimsical smile, "Because they decide to!"

When I pressed him on the matter, he became quite serious and told me that he wasn't kidding. He pointed out that, according to Heisenberg's Theory of Indeterminacy, it was as though each atom had a mind of its own.

How strange!

We who were so sure that the physical universe was nothing more than a gigantic machine that operated according to fixed and stable laws now must grapple with a whole new understanding of the nature of things. We are finding that the world just isn't quite like we thought it was. And what we are discovering suggests that, even at the most rudimentary level of the physical universe, there is something that has a trace of the volitional and is capable of responding to the Spirit of God.

One of the most controversial thinkers of twentieth-century Catholicism, Pierre Teilhard de Chardin, picked up this discovery and gave it religious significance. This theologian and anthropologist outlined a comprehensive view of the development of the universe that has proven to be both insightful and strange. What most of us find intriguing is that Teilhard found a basis for claiming that spiritual forces are at work in the most basic elements of the physical universe.

Teilhard's writings, censored by church officials, were published under the auspices of his atheistic friend, Aldous Huxley. In his books Teilhard brought together in a unified worldview the findings of the laws of physical sciences, discoveries of anthropology, theories about the history and destiny of the cosmos, and biblical teachings. The vision that he gave us of the nature and destiny of the universe and the insights into the history and destiny of the cosmos are brilliant. Even those who have sought to refute his theories could not help but admire his genius.[1]

According to Teilhard, love formed the universe, and love is even now working through all of nature to create the kingdom of God. The universe has a purpose. The *eschaton* (theological term that refers to that final end of history when all things will be fully re-created according to God's will) will be the triumph of love throughout the cosmos.

Love, said Teilhard, is that force that unites and brings things together. Love is that presence that gives coherence to things and creates order out of chaos. Picking up a biblical theme, Teilhard declared that God is love and that the Scriptures tell us that God is the One who holds everything in the cosmos together:

> For by Him all things were created that are in heaven and that are on earth, visible and invisible, whether thrones or dominions or principalities or powers. All things were created through Him and for Him. And He is before all things, and in Him all things consist. (Colossians 1:16–17)

Teilhard believed that it is really God's love that unites the electrons with protons and neutrons. He claimed that God is the One who brought the tiniest particles of matter together to form atoms. And, according to Teilhard, God's love brings atoms together to form the next highest form of matter, molecules.

This process of bringing things together—which Teilhard claimed is facilitated by the love of God—continues until all the matter in the cosmos is created and the material universe with its stars and galaxies is set in place. This creative process is still going on, according to Teilhard, and matter is still being formed out of the gasses in the nebula. Teilhard would say, if he were still with us, that God in His love is still at work spinning and creating throughout "expanding" time and space. And behind everything is the spiritual presence of God's love.

Out of the physical universe, says Teilhard, emerges the biosphere. Love brings together the inanimate and through it, generates the organic. Life is also created by love—by the God who is love. According to Scripture, "All things were made through Him, and without Him nothing was made that was made. In Him was life, and the life was the light of men" (John 1:3–4).

But the process does not end there. Life comes together under the creative influence of love and, in time, gives birth to the peculiar intelligence that is evident in the human race. Teilhard calls this the noosphere. Mind is created out of matter and there emerges in the universe a special family of creatures who are capable of exercising significant control over what goes on in the biosphere. With love, the latest creation of God's love— humanity—can live in harmony with the rest of nature. There can be a new kind of oneness or fellowship with nature. God calls us to unite all of nature in hymns of praise that will glorify God and express His will.

But this human family is also capable of sin. That is, we who make up this family called the human race *can* live counter to God. Because we in the noosphere have minds and wills that can deliberately direct what goes on in the biosphere, it is within our power to disrupt the unity and balance that the God of love has established. We set asunder what God has joined together.

It is this sinful potentiality that has been the basis of the ecological disaster that now confronts us. We who were given the capacity to express love in creation and to participate with God in maintaining His universe have disobeyed our calling. We who have been charged to share with Him in lifting up all of nature to that higher stage, which Teilhard calls the Christosphere, have turned from this mission and used our Godgiven power to tear apart what God has put together. We, who were created to be sons and daughters of the God who makes things one, have become the agents of the powers of darkness and have joined the Evil One in wreaking havoc on God's creation.

But Teilhard is convinced that the God who has been at work throughout the cosmos from the beginning of time will rescue His disrupted creation and lift it up to what it was meant to be. It is to that end, contends Teilhard, that God sent His Son into the world. Jesus, whom Teilhard calls "the Omega Man," breaks into history and initiates the salvation process. The Son of God infuses sinful humanity with the agape love of His Father and in them creates the new Adam and Eve. Those of us who give ourselves over to the Son and are transformed into agents of God's love will, says Teilhard, be the means for rescuing His disrupted and polluted creation. We will become fellow laborers together with Christ (1 Corinthians 3:9) in expressing God's love throughout all of creation and lifting up nature to its destiny as an expression of "the fullness of God."

Teilhard sees Christians as people of *shalom*. God's love, expressed through us, is designed to rescue His suffering creation (Romans 8:19–23) and to initiate the *shalom* that was meant to be when He brought it into being in the beginning.

LOVE VS. THE WILL TO POWER

As Teilhard develops his theology of creation, he makes one very bold move that deserves special consideration. He rejects the commonly accepted theories of evolution as defined by Charles Darwin and Herbert Spencer. These theories of evolution, according to Teilhard, glorify conflict and power rather than God's love. Darwin and Spencer, he points out, make the struggles for survival the basis for all progress.

With Darwin and Spencer, each species of life reproduces until it taxes the resources necessary for survival. Then, in the face of shortages, the process of "natural selection" begins. The various members of the species start to compete with each other for the limited resources necessary for survival. And in this life and death competition, the "fittest" survive and reproduce, leaving the unfit to wither and die. This process of natural selection, contend Darwin and Spencer, insures that the quality of the species will gradually improve. Eventually each constantly developing species evolves into a new and higher form of life, and a new species is born.

In this theory of evolution, conflict is made into a virtue. And as existentialist philosopher Friedrich Nietzsche understood, the survival of the fittest really translates into the survival of the most powerful.

The theories of Darwin and Spencer soon became an ideology for politics and economics. For those who advocated pure *laissez-faire* capitalism, this doctrine of evolution seemed to justify the selfish ruthlessness of the robber barons and the conscienceless exploitation by industrialists. If unbridled competition was the law of nature and the guarantor of progress, then any government interference with these captains of industry would be intolerable. Exploitation of the natural environment went along with exploitation of workers.

Milton Keynes, who gives classical expression to capitalism, states the attitudes engendered by evolution this way:

> For at least another hundred years we must pretend to ourselves and to every one that fair is foul and foul is fair; for foul is useful and fair is not. Avarice and

usury and precaution must be our gods for a little longer still. For only they can lead us out of the tunnel of economic necessity into daylight.[2]

TEILHARD'S ALTERNATIVE

Teilhard opposes Darwin and Spencer's explanation of progress. Consequently, he also opposes the ideology of pure *laissez-faire* capitalism. He refuses to put power on the throne. Teilhard contends that Darwin and Spencer not only contradict the message of the Bible but run counter to what he observed in his scientific investigations of nature.[3]

What is basically going on out there in nature, according to Teilhard, is not so much a testimony to destructive competition as it is an expression of God's love. He contends that cooperation, rather than competition, is the basis of emerging life and biological progress. Through the development of harmonious relationships, rather than power-play conflicts, gains are made both on the biophysical level and on the societal level. Cooperation rather than competition is what makes things better in this world.

Teilhard claims that the driving force that encourages cooperative relationships between species is none other than the love of God. It is God, says Teilhard, who is at work in and through all things. He claims that God gives increasing coherence to everything and every creature in the universe (Colossians 1:17).

There is great significance in Teilhard's abandonment of the evolutionary models of Darwin and Spencer. The doctrines of evolution that extolled the power to dominate and to control the resources of nature are doctrines that have contributed greatly to the demise of the earth's well-being. A theologically and biblically based alternative that is harmonious with science could alter the modern consciousness. It could provide an important contribution to a new mind-set that makes living in harmonious cooperation with the rest of nature a dominant virtue. It could help turn things around and reverse the trend toward an ecological apocalypse.

If the *shalom* of God and the peaceable kingdom of Isaiah 11 are to become real, then new ways of thinking must be established. With some help from St. Francis and Teilhard de Chardin, we just might make it.

8

PREACHING OURSELVES GREEN IN THE FACE

Getting the Church into New Modes of Thinking

When I was just twenty-one years old, I was already out on the preaching circuit. Small churches, located for the most part in South Jersey, would have me come and fill the pulpit when they could not find a "regular preacher."

One hot July Sunday, one of these interesting but very small congregations had me as the guest minister. I had been promised an honorarium of fifty dollars plus a dinner at the home of the wealthiest member.

After the service, my hostess waited for me patiently as I greeted people at the door. Finally, when everyone else had left, she came up to me and told me that I would be eating at her house.

I followed her outside, got into her brand new Cadillac, and settled down comfortably into the posh front passenger seat. The air-conditioned automobile was a welcome relief from the oppressive heat.

As I settled down into what promised to be a blissful ride, my hostess complimented my sermon by telling me, "We need more preaching like that in these last days."

I am not quite sure what I said in response, but I mumbled something. It really didn't matter. She was into her rap on "living in the last days" and did not need a response in order to continue. She pointed out to me that the "signs of the times" were everywhere evident and that there was omnipresent evidence that the world was coming to an end. What was tragic, she pointed out, was that there weren't many preachers like me around to warn people of the impending disaster.

I was pleased to be included among the "good guys," but I was curious as to exactly what she considered to be the marks of good preaching for these last days.

She was happy to tell me. "Good preaching," she said, "is preaching that makes people aware of how bad things are getting. Good sermons are sermons that tell people that the troubles we read about on the front pages of the paper are signs that the end is near and that we had better be ready. Faithful servants of God are the preachers who explain to their people how things will get worse and worse until Christ comes and puts an end to it all."

When we got to her home, which also was air-conditioned, she ushered me to a restful, leather-covered chair. Commenting on how tired I must be, she pushed a button on the side of the chair that set off a vibration. And, as I sat there being pleasantly massaged by the tingling sensations of the chair, she went on with her "prophetic" tirade.

"Yes!" she said. "We really are living in the last days. The work of Satan has made life nothing but trials and tribulations for the people of God." She went on to moan, "Oh, how we people of God have to suffer. Oh, what we have to go through as the end draws near."

As I sat there in that cooled room, feeling from head to toe the pleasant massage of that wonderful chair, and smelling what had to be a roasting turkey, I thought to myself, *If this is what the sufferings of the last days are all about, bring them on! Bring them on!*

This good woman (and she *was* good) was like so many in the church who think that the world is falling apart and that there is really nothing we can or should do about it. She had adopted a particular version of premillennial theology in which human efforts to deter the encroaching influences of Satan accomplish nothing.

Those who hold this opinion suggest that all we Christians can do is tarry patiently until the trumpet sounds and the Lord returns to set everything right again. This kind of thinking often promotes a kind of passive quietism that makes being a Christian nothing more than a quest for a personal holiness that will render us ready for "that great day."

Such theological thinking can be detrimental because it disengages Christians from those activities designed to improve society and, in the case of our discussion, from participating in those social programs designed to save the environment. What is worse is that this kind of theology can get people to throw caution to the wind and act irresponsibly. It becomes too easy for them to say to themselves, "What difference does it make if I'm not careful about preserving the environment? No matter what I do, the world will just get worse and worse until He returns, so I might as well enjoy what God has put here on earth for me to enjoy and not worry about the social consequences."

Thinking like this creates a Christian version of "eat, drink, and be merry." After all, if there is nothing that can be done to alter the disintegrating course of history, why not enjoy life while we still have it?

THE NEED FOR RESPONSIBLE PREACHING

It is no surprise to me that those evangelical preachers who make a big thing out of this kind of premillennialist theology are also the preachers who seem least concerned about environmental issues and the impending ecological disaster. Personal salvation that fosters personal holiness seems to be the limit of their concern.

Some of these preachers, like Hal Lindsey, can even point to a coming ecological holocaust as a kind of "good news." They see it as a "sign" that the second coming of Christ is at hand. And they greet the news of a disintegrating environment with a shout of "Maranatha!"

Once when I was explaining to a group of teenagers at a youth conference how our growing appetite for beef was leading to ecological destruction, I was accused by one well-meaning preacher of being in the spirit of Antichrist. Alluding to 1 Timothy 4:1–4, he pointed out that in the "last days" the spirit of the Evil One would be expressed through those who would command people to "abstain from meats."

It did no good to try to convince him otherwise. I claimed that I really was *not* against the eating of meat. I tried to tell him that I was only asking that our meat consumption be *limited*. I pointed out that we had to prevent the wholesale destruction of rain forests by eliminating the need for more and more grazing land for beef cattle. But he remained undeterred in his accusation.

There are pulpiteers who even claim that there really is no environmental problem. These often sincere preachers claim that all of this talk about global warming and pollution is nothing more than part of the plot of some ungodly "liberals" who are agents of Satan trying to bring down this great nation of ours.

According to their reasoning, the measures to save the environment are so economically costly that they will make our industries less competitive on the world market. These preachers contend that if we do all the things that the environmentalists are demanding, we will end up with production processes that are too expensive. Then what we produce will be too high-priced to sell in a marketplace where other countries produce and sell goods more cheaply. The result will be the collapse of the nation that, they say, is God's primary agent for the Christian missionary enterprise and is humanity's best hope for the future.

I hope that at this point I do not have to defend myself against such absurdities. Furthermore, I trust that we are all aware that this nation, even this world, would be more likely to collapse not because of measures designed to protect the environment but because of the lack of such measures. I hope that most of us are beyond the point where we believe that God is somehow dependent on the

United States of America to establish His kingdom here on earth.

MY POSITION

Suspicions to the contrary, I believe in the premillennial return of Christ. On the other hand, I certainly do *not* work on the details of predicting just how and when the Second Coming will occur. Whenever the discussion focuses on such things, I like to say, "I'm on the welcoming committee, not the program committee."

I also want to make it clear that neither am I a postmillennialist who believes that through our efforts alone the kingdom of God will become a historical reality. I am not suggesting that the perfect world will be established without the return of Christ. Quite to the contrary!

I believe that the new heaven and the new earth will come in its fullness only with an apocalyptic return of Jesus. *He* will establish *shalom* at His coming. On that great day, He will put an end to the destructive violence that now plagues the earth. The second coming of Christ will signal the complete deliverance of creation from its present bondage to corruption.

What must be made clear is that each of us has a responsibility to do something about our polluted and trashed creation right *now*. In anticipation of His coming, we must go to work today and participate with Him in caring for all parts of His creation, making our contribution to the work which He will complete on the day of His coming (Philippians 1:6). The Bible tells us that the time is at hand to labor with Christ in initiating the cleanup.

God Working Through His Church

God has already taken on the task of planetary salvation and environmental renewal through us, and He is doing it here and now. What is being accomplished in a limited fashion in the present will become increasingly evident as we pass through the "last days." The church is to play a key role as God carries out His redemptive plan for His cosmos. The Scriptures tell us that God has "put all things under His feet, and gave Him to be head over all things to the church" (Ephesians 1:22).

The church is His instrument for rescuing His polluted world, and He will make it new again (Revelation 21:5). The people who make up Christ's body are the primary agents for His commitment to fulfill His plans for the future of our planet.

We know that the God who even now is working through His people to make all things good (Romans 8:28) will not leave us hanging. He will reenter history in power and glory. And He will complete the work which He initiated through His church. The church will accomplish *something* of His saving work. But it is only when He returns and joins our feeble efforts, that we can expect the defeat of the ecological evils of our time by the goodness of God. Between now and then, the church must be about the business He will complete.

Stirring Our Emotions

Seldom, if ever, do we hear sermons on the environment. Those who do deliver messages on this subject may well be held suspect of being theologically offbeat. Most commonly, they are accused of being part of the New Age movement. But I suppose the main problem with those who preach such sermons is their seeming inability to stir us to action. These ecologically conscious preachers are themselves often quite agitated about the condition of the world. They can show real anger over what we are doing to the atmosphere, to the oceans, and to the rain forests. They are able to rant and rave about the future of "spaceship earth" as they call on us to "do something" to turn things around. But the one thing they don't seem to be able to do is to tap our emotions. They cannot get us to weep over what we have done to nature.

We shake our heads in rational dismay over what we hear. We nod in approval when we are told that "earth care" should be a priority on the agenda of the church. But most of these preachers who call on us to save the environment cannot set our hearts on fire.

Environmental issues must be much more than concerns which arise from rational reflection if there is to be a movement created to cure the ills of creation. Emotion starts movements; reason is not enough. Facts and figures that give evidence of the impending ecological disaster are necessary, but if we are going to be moved to action, we must feel the travail of creation.

We all knew that racial discrimination was wrong, but not until Martin Luther King, Jr., drew the hearts of white people into empathy with their African-American brothers and sisters was a movement born. White people, listening to the brilliant messages of King, felt something of the plight of the oppressed. And once they began to feel what African-American people suffered day in and day out, the old structures of Jim Crow were deemed intolerable, and change was inevitable.

World hunger aroused compassion when pictures of starving children in Africa began to appear on our television screens. The haunting eyes of emaciated children seemed to peer right into our hearts, and our emotional reactions to those children stirred us to action. *Feeling* their pain, not merely knowing the statistics, motivated us to try to do something for these victims of poverty.

But when it comes to environmental issues, we have been unable to stir emotions. The facts are startling and the predictions are ominous, but neither elicit the kind of *feelings* that can be translated into activism.

If we cannot get people to feel something about what is happening because of our careless disregard for creation, then they will remain complacent. If we cannot stir them emotionally by helping them to relate to the sufferings of creatures that roam this planet, then we will not be able to elicit the kind of response that will help the animals and save endangered species.

OPEN DOOR TO OTHER RELIGIONS

My concern is that if we fail to develop a *biblically based* theology of nature that fosters feeling for nature, then other religions and New Age gurus will move in to offer alternative belief systems that do. If the church cannot teach the citizens of our century how to enter into the sufferings of creation, those false prophets who play with the occult will. Then charlatans will be the only ones to offer people a spiritual basis for being pro-actively responsible for their environment.

Already, many are finding in Buddhism what seems to be a valid basis to respect and reverence nature. The religious philosophy of Buddha appears to offer a comprehensive worldview that invites believers to empathize with everyone of God's creatures. In the Buddhist scriptures, followers are urged to take on the kind of consciousness which was incarnated in the "compassion-ate Buddha" and make it their own. Since Christian theologians and preachers have not articulated any alter-native, "seekers" seem inclined toward this religion of the East.

In the struggle for the minds and hearts of this gen-eration, we cannot yield anything to Buddhism or any version of the New Age movement. We cannot give ground on this incredibly pertinent issue. If some kind of empathy with nature is essential to the development of a mind-set that can rescue dying creation, then we must show that the biblical message meets this need. We must, therefore, carefully develop the implications of what we know about how Jesus related to nature. And, until we come up with some more solid alternatives, the perspectives of St. Francis and Teilhard ought to provide some of the inspiration for our preaching.

LISTENING TO THE ECO-FEMINISTS

As we evangelicals seek to develop a new consciousness and a workable theology to address the urgent needs of creation-care, we may have to pay attention to many who regard us as their enemies. As we try to rethink our attitudes toward nature, we may have to learn some re-spect for theologies and belief systems that we have hitherto dismissed with a wave of the hand. In our at-tempt to equip Christians to deal with contemporary is-sues in such a way that concerned secularists will turn to the church for hope and help, we may have to open our own ears to some new voices.

One such source of teaching is the feminist movement. The spokespersons for feminist theology have argued that there are deep historical connections between male-centered thinking and the destructive dispositions that have led to the spoiling of nature. They argue that our definition of what constitutes a "manly" man must change if the kind of humanity that is compassionately related to nature is to develop. The feminists argue that the attitudes that have led men to dominate and exploit women are the same attitudes that have led them to dominate and exploit nature.

I remember as a boy listening to our Sunday school teacher telling us how macho it was to hunt. He talked about how shooting down a buck was proof that a boy had become a man. He told us that he had the antlers of the first buck he had killed on the wall in his den to remind him of that important time when he had showed everyone that he wasn't a sissy kid anymore. I sat there listening with wonder and awe and hoped that someday I would be able to do something that "brave" and grown up. A girl in our Sunday school class asked if it didn't make him feel even just a little bad to hurt the deer and make it cry.

"Deer don't cry," I remember him saying with a sneer. "It's just like a girl to worry about something like that."

We all laughed at that girl, and the boys in the class made quite a display of mocking her sentimentality. So often boys try to show off their toughness by putting down displays of sensitivity and by identifying with those men who do not have such "mushy" feelings.

As I look back on that little episode, I now realize that it was just a small part of my socialization into manhood. And when I reflect on what manhood meant to me then, I shudder just a little. What I was learning about maleness that day was just what the feminists contend is wrong.

Men, say the feminists, are taught to establish their identity by exercising power and domination over the rest of creation—and that, of course, includes women. Feminists point out that men are always looking for trophies that will prove them to be conquering heroes. Men, say the feminists, consider the antlers of deer to be displays of their manhood and, in like manner, they also enjoy showing off their submissive women as evidence of their power to dominate. As long as males are brought up to establish their identity through conquests, neither women nor the rest of nature will be safe.

As I reflect on feminist thinking, I realize that there is obvious truth to it. I think about guys I knew in my college days who moved so quickly from one girl to the next. There was no love involved. As a matter of fact, they bragged about how they were able to fool these young women into thinking that they loved them so they could hustle them into bed. They seemed quite proud of the lines they had developed and the smoothness with which they used them to seduce women. Not only was there no feeling in what those men did, but they gloried in the fact that there was no feeling. What was important was the conquest. And if the girl had been a virgin—all the better! Virginity was a *real* trophy. To be the first one *really* proved something.

In retrospect, the attitude of my Sunday school teacher about hunting a deer to be a trophy of his manhood and the attitudes of those adolescent males had a great deal in common. What is *Playboy* magazine if not a guidebook for insecure "boys" who want to see what kind of "girls" they have to have in order to prove that they are men? Exploitation of the sacred is a virtue in our male chauvinistic sexist society, and it is this disposition that destroys everything and everybody who doesn't belong to the "old boy" network.

If nature is to be saved, then men have to be delivered from the models of manliness that have thus far guided the socialization of so many of them. Men have to learn that maturity requires taking on some qualities which they hitherto have deemed fit only for women. They must learn sensitivity and gentleness. They must learn empathy and the joy of yielding in love. They must learn how to feel in new ways that have hitherto been considered "soft" and sentimental. Only a new breed of men, imbued with such qualities, can be trusted with a creation which gives every evidence of being fragile and easily hurt.

Jesus had all of these traits that our macho culture has labeled feminine. He knew how to cry—even when people could see Him (John 11:33–36). He was one of those tender people who enjoyed cuddling little children (Matthew 19:13–14). He was a sensitive person who could always pick out of a crowd anyone who was hurting (Matthew 9:20–22) or feeling shut out (Luke 19:1–6). The word *sweet* could easily have been applied to this rugged Galilean. And Jesus would not have considered being called "nice" an insipid label. The church would do well to consider what it really means to tell its male members to be like Jesus.

But if men are to learn how to take on this new kind of maleness, *women must teach them*. If men are to enjoy this new kind of humanness, then women must show them how. And if men are to be delivered from offensive, destructive, and dominating ways, then women, who are much less inclined toward such behavior, must be their tutors.

Ironically, evangelical men are often reluctant to learn anything from women. They readily quote Scripture to make the case that women shouldn't even try to teach them anything. Now, at a time when men need help the most, they are making a major case to justify not having to listen.

I contend that not only should women be allowed to be preachers and teachers, but if the environment is to be rescued from destruction, men *need* to have women in such roles. Those who would be first must become last, and those who would be teachers must become learners.

A NEW CHRISTIAN LIFE-STYLE

Lastly, the church that is going to be a responsible steward of creation and help to develop a new humanity fit for our threatened planet must teach its people a whole new life-style. And spelling out that life-style is a difficult, controversial task that church leaders have generally avoided.

Just after high school, I had a brief excursion into a Bible college education. The few months I spent in Bible college proved to be some of the most valuable time of my entire educational life. To be frank about it, in Bible college I really learned what is in the Scriptures.

At the time, the thing that bothered me most about Bible college was a pledge card I had to sign. This particular Bible college wanted its students to maintain a life-style that would provide a good testimony before "the world." I was angered by that pledge card because when I signed it, I had to promise that I would not dance, drink alcoholic beverages, go to movies, and (believe it or not) go to bowling alleys. You see, there is beer drinking in some bowling alleys, and people who might see you coming out of such places could possibly think that you had been there to drink instead of just to bowl.

I resented that pledge because I didn't think the administration had any right to prescribe how *I* should live.

I was wrong!

Upon careful reflection, I now think that Christians in the church have the right to spell out for each other the norms of acceptable Christian behavior. I now think that it is perfectly legitimate for the people of God to discern what is godly behavior in our world and to expect that behavior from the members of the church.

What still bothers me about that pledge is that the marks of the Christian life-style which it spelled out were too limited and did not move beyond personal piety. In my opinion, that pledge majored in minors. Nowadays, I believe that Christians ought to sign pledges on weightier issues (Matthew 23:23). They should be a testimony to an irresponsible society as to how God expects us to live. Among those things that should be prescribed in a pledge for those who call themselves Christians are the requisites to be caretakers of the environment and instruments for the renewal of a polluted creation. I would like to see a new church covenant for members to sign. Allow me to make a suggestion as to how such a covenant might read:

THE COVENANT

I commit myself to a life of personal purity and spirituality.

I commit myself to being a co-laborer together with Christ in rescuing all of creation from injustices, pollution, and other works of the Evil One.

I believe in the truths of the Apostles' Creed. Therefore, I believe that God created both the heavens and the earth and all the creatures therein. I will not kill animals needlessly nor for entertainment. Instead, I will care for animals and assure food and shelter for all creatures for which I have accepted responsibility.

I promise to be loyal to the church and to encourage the local congregation to which I belong to be faithful in declaring God's salvation both for persons and for the structures of society.

To achieve the aims of this covenant, I commit myself to regular prayer and to a support group that will keep me faithful to its principles.

Disciples of Jesus must set a new standard for living. It is not legalism to set down expectations for church members. It is only legalistic when we make living by those expectations the condition for salvation.

Faithfulness to these expectations cannot be achieved by individuals working things out alone. In order to be faithful, each of us needs to belong to a support group.

Every Tuesday morning at 7:00 A.M., I meet with three other men. This is my support group. I know that without these friends praying for me, correcting me, encouraging me, and teaching me, I could not even come close to the calling to be a faithful disciple of Christ. What I need, I believe every Christian needs. Any one of us who is committed to living out the kind of discipleship outlined in this suggested covenant needs the support of others. We need close friends who know us and will hold us as individuals accountable to commitments we have made.

Let it be said loud and clear: We are saved by *grace*—not because we adhere to a set of rules. We are saved because of what Jesus did for us on the cross—not because we have been environmentally responsible or have worked for social justice. Our salvation is a gift. It is not something we can earn.

Now that we have carefully delineated the basis of salvation, let us go on and spell out the cost of discipleship. Let us teach the people of the church that they can show their gratitude to God for the gift of His Son by living in responsible obedience to His will. This certainly includes living in a way that does not hurt the rest of creation. It means living simply so that others can simply live.

9

MISSIONS WITH THE WORLD IN MIND

New Dimensions for Christian Outreach

*E*nvironmental concerns have stimulated a whole new brand of missionary work. Some respond to the Great Commission by going to the Third World with a vision for alleviating the problems that have been created by our abusive exploitation of natural resources. A notable example of this new missionary vision is the work of Tom Woodard of the United States and Cesar Lopez of the Dominican Republic.

These two men joined together to form Floresta, a missionary organization whose calling is to plant trees in the Third World. Starting in the Dominican Republic, Lopez and Woodard have committed themselves to a program of reforestation. This past year, their mission-ary organization planted over five million trees. This makes Floresta the single largest reforestation program in any Caribbean nation. In addition to the five million forest trees, Floresta workers also planted more than fifty thousand fruit trees and seven hundred thousand coffee trees.

While restoring life to land that was on the verge of becoming a desert, the Floresta missionaries have simul-taneously created jobs for scores of poor people in the Dominican Republic. Their tree nursery, located about fifty miles north of Santo Domingo, the capital city, pro-vides decent-paying jobs for many Dominicans who hitherto had scant means for supporting their families or living with dignity.

But no one in the Dominican Republic is more grate-ful for the work of these missionaries than the hundreds of farmers who have become participants in the Floresta programs. They have found a new way of increasing their incomes while, at the same time, participating in restoring their country to its former splendor. Typical of such farmers is a man named Don Paulino.

Don Paulino used to be a mountain *campesino*—a man who made his living by cutting down trees for making charcoal. Most people in the Dominican Repub-lic cook on charcoal stoves, and the production and sale of charcoal provides one of the few means of income for the poor.

After clearing the land of trees, Don Paulino would plant traditional food crops. But the beans that he planted were unsuited for growing on the steep hills and mountainsides of his country. Each year, tropical rains washed away the valuable topsoil and leached nutrients from the uncovered land. The soil from Don

Paulino's farm, along with soil from his neighbors' farms, washed downstream where it clogged the turbines of the only hydroelectric dam in the country. The silt also suffocated the marine fisheries along the shoreline, making it almost impossible for fishermen to catch enough fish to make their living.

The Floresta missionaries reached out to Don Paulino and spent many hours explaining to him how his farming habits were destroying his country, increasing poverty for others, and putting him on a path toward personal economic disaster. They showed him how each year his increasingly worn-out land would produce less and less food, leaving him with a smaller and smaller income.

Don Paulino was both an intelligent man and a good Christian. He quickly understood from Scripture that he had a responsibility to God to take care of creation. The Floresta missionaries explained how deforestation not only hurt his own community but affected people around the world. He learned how deforestation removes nature's carbon dioxide absorber and creates the greenhouse effect. He saw how farming procedures in the rural hills of a small country in the Caribbean can have devastating effects on the world's weather.

With the help of Floresta's revolving loan fund and training program, Don Paulino was able to progress from growing rows of beans to planting trees. Using a planned planting and harvesting scheme that plants more trees on the land than are cut down, the farm is producing citrus fruit and fuel wood that provides Don Paulino and his family with a good and stable income. As he pays back the loan that enabled him to secure the land he now uses and to care for his family during the difficult transitional years, he is making it possible for other farmers to borrow money and do the same thing he did. Within a couple of years, Floresta will have almost one thousand Dominican farmers in the program that has given hope to Don Paulino.

As you travel south down the main highway of the Dominican Republic, you cannot help but notice the three mountains that dominate the vista. Two of them are devastated and bare because of deforestation. But the one in the middle is lush with green trees. This middle mountain is a testimony to Floresta, a declaration of the kingdom of God, and a positive statement about a Savior who came into the world to make all things new.

Floresta's accomplishments should serve as a model for mission boards everywhere.[1] Some have already taken a cue from this enterprise and initiated programs of their own. Pat Robertson of the "700 Club" has sponsored a missionary program that has planted more than three million trees. In Africa and the Caribbean, some forward-looking mission schools sponsored by the American Baptist Convention are teaching indigenous peoples to support themselves by working in reforestation programs.

Christians who support missionary enterprise should prod those agencies to promote ecologically responsible programs. If all the agricultural missionaries made ecological concerns a high priority, if every church taught every member to plant just one tree each year in the name of Jesus, we would begin to see a difference.

The church must take the initiative in these matters; help is unlikely to come from any other sector of the societal systems of the Third World. In most of these countries, the governments are too unstable and too poor to focus much attention on what is happening to the environment. Most Third World presidents and parliaments have their hands full just staying in power.

Leaders in such tenuous situations are unlikely to promote policies to save the environment.

The private sector in Third World countries is often too oriented toward maximizing profits to make a major contribution to saving the environment. In reality, many businesses and industries relocate to the Third World because they want to escape the regulations against pollution in places like the United States and Western Europe. These multinational corporations often make matters worse.

That leaves the church. It alone has both the resources and the moral imperatives to promote economic practices that can make the difference in the poor and struggling countries of the world. Indigenous Christians linked with their brothers and sisters in wealthy countries could come up with programs that might begin to restore our messed-up creation to its original glory.

But Christian people will not be inspired to take such bold action unless they have an understanding of the mission of the church and an interpretation of the biblical revelations that provide imperatives for ecological responsibility.

Whatever else may be promoted by the theology now envisioned, there must be a strong emphasis on a concept of salvation. The gospel must be presented according to Jesus. Our Lord did not preach a doctrine of salvation that was limited to what would happen to a particular individual who *might* choose to believe in Him and trust in Him for eternal life. But as important as it is to declare that Jesus came to save those who join His church, it is essential that we do not make this emphasis the whole message. We must also declare in word and in deed that God sent His Son to save the whole cosmos (John 3:16). We must make the church aware that we share in the mission of Jesus. We must make every believer understand that missions is the declaration and extension of the kingdom of God. They must grasp the fact that the kingdom of God is to be, among many other things, a restored creation. Only when the church prays with this kind of perspective for the kingdom to come on earth as it is in heaven will it make environmental renewal a part of the missionary enterprise. Only when concern for *all* of creation is made a vital part of the message of those who preach and teach will the church give legitimacy to a new breed of missionaries who have good news about what God wills for all that He has made.

COTTAGE INDUSTRIES AND ENVIRONMENTAL RESPONSIBILITY

While a great deal of the devastation of the environment in Third World countries is carried out by multinational corporations, most of it is the result of the actions of poor people who feel that they have no alternatives. The poor in countries like the Dominican Republic and Haiti understand what their "slash and burn" farming techniques are doing to the land. The problem, they point out, is that they can find no other ways to provide financial support for their families.

Jobs are incredibly scarce in such poor nations. In the Dominican Republic, more than 40 percent of the work force is either underemployed or completely unemployed. In Haiti, the figure is more like 80 percent. Telling people in such countries that they have to give up cutting down trees, which usually is their only means of income, is both ludicrous and futile. Actually there is a law in the Dominican Republic prohibiting the cutting down of trees, but it has little effect.

There are Christians in the United States who are not indifferent to this scenario of poverty in the Third World, and they have decided to do something about it. One such group of concerned Christians has put together a missionary organization called Opportunities International. Based just outside of Chicago, this missionary society creates jobs among the poor in the Third World. It is committed to developing small businesses and cottage industries which are income-producing alternatives to the "slash and burn" agricultural practices that are devastating the Third World. The work of Opportunities International is carried out by making very small loans (usually for one hundred to five hundred dollars) to entrepreneurs who need hard capital to carry out their plans. This unique missionary organization has helped to develop thousands of small businesses and cottage industries and has created tens of thousands of new jobs. We cannot simply say to the poor of Third World countries, "Stop cutting down trees!" We have to provide alternatives. And Opportunities International is doing just that.[2]

The administration of Eastern College, where I teach sociology, took note of what Opportunities International was doing. With the help of Al Whittikers, the man most responsible for developing this creative missionary organization, Eastern started a graduate program to train a new generation of missionaries to be the catalysts for ecologically sound entrepreneurial ventures around the world. Scores of graduates from Eastern are already out on the mission field, serving the poor by helping them start businesses and cottage industries that indigenous people will own and run. Inspired by the ideas outlined by E. F. Schumacher in his book *Small Is Beautiful*, these "Entrepreneurs for Biblical Justice" (as they sometimes call themselves) are trying to utilize what Schumacher calls "appropriate technology" to provide means of production and income that do not harm the environment.[3] Graduates of Eastern's program know that the best way to fight poverty in the Third World is by creating jobs for the poor. And they also know that those jobs must be in production schemes that maintain a healthy ecological equilibrium.

Perhaps the most innovative of the array of programs inspired by the graduate program at Eastern College are the businesses and cottage industries which use recycled materials. By using junk and trash as raw materials, previously unemployed people are able to produce a line of products that sell well both to indigenous peoples and among those who live in "developed" countries.[4]

In the Dominican Republic, there is a factory that makes sandals out of discarded automobile tires. In Malaysia, scores of poor people are weaving strips of rubber from tires into matting for pick-up trucks and for flooring in machine shops. In Africa, aluminum cans become a variety of kitchen utensils and toys.

In these, and in a host of other creative ventures, Eastern students are learning ways to pick up the junk that seems to be omnipresent and turn it into things that are useful. Programs like this offer great hope for a new kind of socially relevant missionary work and must be encouraged and replicated.

A GREEN PARTY FOR CHRISTIANS

Something that is *not* happening yet but that I think should happen is the creation of a Christian green party.

Alongside the traditional political parties, environmentally concerned people have formed green parties in England, France, Germany, Holland, Belgium, and Italy, as well as in the Scandinavian countries. On rare occasions they have been able to get candidates elected to office. However, their real purpose is not so much to gain political power as to make sure that environmental concerns are constantly a part of the discussions in parliaments and of the platforms of other political parties.

Green party people make certain that decision makers are aware of the plight of helpless animals. They speak up to protect nature from those who too readily ignore its destruction at the hands of the uninformed and the uncaring. They raise the awareness of political candidates.

I do not think the church itself ought to sponsor a green party. Personally, I think it is a mistake for the church to ally itself with any political party. But what the church as a whole should not do, individual, environmentally conscious members of the church can and ought to do. In Europe, green parties have become bastions of leftists and Marxists. Sadly, very few Christians are in the ranks. Consequently, environmental concerns often become the domain of those who are cynical about Christianity.

I do not think we should allow secularists and those opposed to Christianity to become the spokespersons for a cause that is biblically prescribed. Since I am convinced that saving planet earth from pollution and ugliness is God's will, I am also convinced that Christians must be ready to become His agents. As public spokespersons for those who want to liberate the earth from those who would oppress it and misuse it, Christians give evidence that their God is interested in more than what goes on in church. This is an opportunity to let the world know that our God is the cosmic God and that He is interested in one of the major issues of our time.

I am suggesting that individual Christians who share a common concern for rescuing our threatened planet get organized locally. In some instances, it might be a wise strategy to run candidates, but in most cases, that probably would not be the best thing to do. Actually, being an independent party that can throw its endorsement to whichever candidates from the major parties are most supportive of green causes may get the best results. This latter strategy is likely to get everybody in the field vying for the green party endorsement. This will work only if the members of the green party promise to work in the campaign and at the polls for the endorsed candidate.

On the local level, Christians in the green party should address issues that relate to the communities in which they live. They should be concerned with such things as programs of trash collection that make provisions for the recycling of paper, bottles, and cans. They should make sure that environmental issues are properly covered in the curriculum of the public school system. They should work for legislation that would limit, if not outlaw, styrofoam containers at local fast-food establishments. By making environmental issues a local concern, they can most readily achieve concrete action. It is always easier to get things done on the local level than on the state or national level.

I believe in a "trickle up" revolution. I believe that what happens on the township level or in the city council is recognized by those on higher levels. I am convinced that movements begin when people, right where they live, decide to make a difference in what is going on around them. What starts on the micro level is soon felt on the macro level. Or, as Jesus told us, if we are faithful in the little things, we will become "rulers" over great things (Matthew 25:21).

Sooner or later, green parties will appear across America. I want Christians to be the *avant garde* this time. In former times, we have not recognized the legitimacy of moral, social movements in time to significantly influence their ideologies. We usually come too late with too little to the causes that really matter. This time, let's get there first. This is God's creation, and we are called to care for it; that is the basis of the coming environmental movement.

These would be just a few of the signs indicating the church is waking up to the challenge which our polluted environment and the impending ecological disaster presents to us. But we are waking up. It will not be long before the creativity, which comes from the Holy Spirit, leads the church to exciting new solutions. I am full of hope.

10

Some New Wine in Old Wineskins

An Invitation to Join with Nature in Worshiping God

Some years ago, I was invited to spend a day with a former student who had taken a job at a camp for "special" children, most of whom were mentally retarded. Part of that day was spent on a nature hike. As I walked with these children, I realized, in part, why they were called "special." They seemed to have an appreciation of nature that had real depth and sensitivity. There was a sense of glee about them as they chased butterflies and touched the bark of trees. Everything their guide pointed out to them was treated with awe and reverence. They were like visitors from another planet to whom the life forms of the forest were wonderful surprises. They were fascinated by things that I had learned to ignore. They experienced nature in ways that I had forgotten. They seemed to delight in the things of God and to enjoy what He had made for them.

Their childlike joy at coming upon daisies and buttercups was infectious, and it was not long before they had reawakened in me a variety of feelings that had been left somewhere in a simpler and less complicated time in my life. The words of Jesus—"Verily I say unto you, whosoever shall not receive the kingdom of God as a little child shall in no wise enter therein" (Luke 18:17)—had a new ring to them. And I could only say thank you to these special children for helping me to break out of the categories of perception that had so limited my vision.

Respect and concern for the environment has to come from this special kind of spiritual sensitivity to nature. Statistics on the depletion rate of the rain forests or the facts about the destruction of the ozone layer won't do it.

Only if we, as a people, once again fall in love with nature and subjectively empathize with the sense of the transcendent that can be encountered there will the careless destruction of the environment distress us. Only if we, in biblical language, "have eyes to see and ears to hear" the sacred presence in the midst of the natural is there any real possibility that we will become caretakers of God's creation as He has called us to be. There is something out there in the forest that we see only "through a glass darkly" which we must come to appreciate "face to face." There is a dimension of reality hidden out there in the hills and the mountains that we know only "in part" which we must come to know "even as also we are known." Only then will we feel the urgency of the need to save the environment and to protect all of those creatures who share it with us.

This kind of heightened consciousness of the sacredness of nature is very much evident among the Amish people who live in Lancaster County, Pennsylvania. My friend and former teaching colleague, William M. Kephart, has carried on extensive studies of this intriguing subculture. He points out that the Amish refuse to use any of the chemical fertilizers which have become so common on farms across America. According to the Amish, using these chemicals poisons the ground. This, they contend, would be sinful since the soil is sacred. In almost Mosaic fashion, they recognize that they stand on holy ground and that the land which they farm has a spiritual quality about it which must be respected. They believe that if we expect the land to give us crops to harvest, we must treat it with some degree of reverence.

In light of what we have come to know about the effect of chemical fertilizers on the soil and how they contaminate our rivers, lakes, and oceans, perhaps we should adopt the attitudes of the Amish.

That same religious disposition toward the land is something I sensed as I read the Russian novels by Fyodor Dostoyevski. Time and time again the characters in these novels talk about the sacredness of the soil of "Mother Russia." These people regularly get down on their hands and knees and kiss the ground to express their grateful love for all of the blessings it provides for them. The characters in these novels seem to recognize a kind of radiant spirituality in the soil and believe that there are special blessings in store for those who are surrendered to its nurturing effects. "Mother Russia," they believe, gives good things to her children.

Something of this same attitude of religious awe is evident also among tribal peoples in Africa. As a visitor, this sense of the sacredness of land became immediately apparent to me.

I went to Africa under the auspices of an American economic development agency with the express purpose of figuring out how to encourage rural Africans to use modern techniques of agriculture. As I tried to find out who owned the land so that I could help set up some experimental farms, I was almost always greeted by confused and questioning eyes. To them, their land was a gift from God to their tribe. It belonged to all their people as a sacred trust, and the idea of its being treated as private property for individual profit was outside their comprehension.

I realized I had witnessed this sense of the holy in nature in those special children on the nature hike, in the characters portrayed in Russian novels, and in the tribal people in Africa. This same sense of holiness appeared in the mystical experiences of St. Francis and in the writings of John Wesley. As I thought about what these men had written, I knew that I had enjoyed something of their experiences. Nature had restored to me something of the miraculous that I had once known in childhood.

I have become increasingly aware of the sacramental character of nature and have come to realize that God's creation is a special means of grace. The psalmist wrote, "Taste and see that the LORD is good" (Psalm 34:8), and I know I'm beginning to understand nature in a new and spiritual way.

As I have read what the Scriptures and the theologians have to say about God's creation, and as I reflect upon my own personal relationships and experiences with nature, I have begun to grasp a new and qualitatively different kind of religious experience. I call it a "religious experience" because the character of this experience is not confined to what Christians know. Instead, this experience is what is known about God through what the theologians call "natural revelation." The first chapter of Romans describes this kind of encounter with God:

> Because what may be known of God is manifest in them, for God has shown it to them. For since the creation of the world His invisible attributes are clearly seen, being understood by the things that are made, even His eternal power and Godhead, so that they are without excuse. (Romans 1:19–20)

This kind of awareness of God is hidden from those who have become too accustomed to viewing nature through eyes conditioned by secular society—eyes blinded to the presence of the spiritual in the midst of the physical.

HAVING EARS TO HEAR

A South Jersey farmer was on a tour of New York City when he stopped his companion and asked, "Do you hear that cricket?"

His companion, a friend of mine, was more than taken back by the question. After all, they were in New York City. They were just off Broadway in the theater district. There were horns blaring and people shouting. There were brakes screeching and car doors slamming. The cacophony was overpowering, almost deafening. And yet this old farmer wanted to know if his friend could hear a cricket.

He stopped, walked a few steps up an alleyway, and motioned his friend to follow him. And there, hiding in a crevice of a brick building was the cricket. How it got there is impossible to say. But it was there. And the farmer from South Jersey had heard its cry. Amidst the clamor and hubbub of the city, this farmer had heard a lone cricket because he had a sensitivity to crickets that came from having heard them sing thousands of nights behind his barn at home. He heard because he had the ears to hear what so many others would never hear. He heard what he was prepared to hear.

When it comes to sensing God's presence in the midst of nature, the same principle holds. We must train ourselves to hear and to see and to feel Him speaking to us through His creation. He is there and waits to be appreciated by those who would obey His words, "Be still, and know that I am God" (Psalm 46:10).

BECOMING A ROYAL PRIESTHOOD

My new realization of what nature is and what it can become has not only challenged me to love nature in such a way as to become its protector, but it has also ushered me into a very enriching kind of devotional life.

The Psalms have become important to me. I no longer view them so much as a source of theology; they are a book of prayers and praise for worship. I have felt deeply their poetic power and their revelation of the subjective character of true worshipers of God. They have begun to lead me into something of the experiences of David who, in his worship of God, overcame aloneness and enjoyed an ecstatic communion with God through nature. In the Psalms, I enter into the mind-set of one who, even though he was by himself as a shepherd boy, experienced companionship and was able to join with nature in worshiping Yahweh.

We humans are by no means the only creatures who can worship God. All of nature was created for this end. The catechism may say that the main purpose of God's people is to worship Him and adore Him forever, but such a calling belongs to all His other creatures too (Psalms 103:20–22; 104).

I increasingly believe that it is a humanistic distortion to think that nature was created by God solely for the benefit of Adam and Eve and their successors. The idea that nature is there simply to provide blessings and gratification for humans seems to me to be more of a manifestation of anthropocentric exaggeration than an expression of how things really are.

Allow me to suggest that all of God's creations were spoken into existence primarily to glorify Him. Consider the possibility that everything that is, both in heaven and on earth, was brought into being mainly to "magnify the Lord" and to "bring honor to His name."

Give some thought to the proposition that we may be selfishly appropriating for our own use what God ordained for His own worship. In other words, when our life-style leads to destroying the environment, we are raising havoc with what God created to worship Him. Furthermore, consider that as one of its most important purposes, stewardship of creation should sustain nature's worshiping capacity. The more I reflect on the Scriptures and the more I sense how God thrills to the adoration He receives from all that He has created, the more I realize that He has given us the awesome responsibility of caring for His creation so that it can go on praising Him until the end of time.

The psalmist certainly believed that the earth and all of its creatures were ordained to worship God. David tried to remind us that nature has this capability:

> The heavens declare the glory of God;
> And the firmament shows His handiwork.
> Day unto day utters speech,
> And night unto night reveals knowledge.
> There is no speech nor language
> Where their voice is not heard.
> Their line has gone out through all the earth,
> And their words to the end of the world.
> In them He has set a tabernacle for the sun,
> Which is like a bridegroom coming
>   out of his chamber,
> And rejoices like a strong man to run its race.
> Its rising is from one end of heaven,
> And its circuit to the other end;
> And there is nothing hid from its heat.
>
>   (Psalm 19:1–6)

And the hymn writer, Robert Grant, picked up this theme when he wrote "O Worship the King:"

> O tell of His might,
> O sing of His grace,
> Whose robe is the light,
> Whose canopy space;
> His chariots of wrath
> The deep thunderclouds form,
> And dark is His path
> On the wings of the storm.
>
> Thy bountiful care
> What tongue can recite?
> It breathes in the air,
> It shines in the light,

It streams from the hills,
It descends to the plain,
And sweetly distills
In the dew and the rain.

(vv. 2–3)

Sin and evil, it can be argued, have perverted nature. The Evil One has lured nature away from its high calling. The violence and death that are seen throughout creation are the result of Satan's work. The Evil One, since he was cast out of heaven, has been at work "binding" all of God's creatures so that they are limited both in what they can do to reveal God to us and in the extent to which they can worship Yahweh. Creation still has a great capacity for revelation and worship, but it is far short of what it was ordained to do "in the beginning."

Consequently, those of us who pollute the earth become partners with Satan in destroying creation's calling and ability to worship God. As our wanton exploitation of nature renders increasing species of animals and plants extinct, there are fewer kinds of praise that can be raised to the Lord. As our willful and wholesale depletion of forests becomes more and more evident, it is also evident that there are fewer and fewer trees that can point upward to God and rustle their leaves in applause to the King of the universe. And as our fuel consumption turns the atmosphere brown with carbons and dirt, and our carelessness results in oil slicks that cover the waters, nature loses much of its capacity to glorify God and to reveal His awesome greatness to all generations (Psalm 79:13).

That nature was meant to glorify God does not preclude its use for the good of the heirs of the first couple. God wants us to enjoy nature and to feast on its fruits (Genesis 1:29–30). But when our God wills us to enjoy nature, He wills us to enjoy it in such a way as to preserve its beauty and to maintain its capacity for glorifying Him. Therefore, when our greed, carelessness, and disregard do permanent damage to creation's beauty and limit its worshipful character, we sin. It even might be said that the violation of nature is a kind of blasphemy in that it is the result of turning nature from the worship of God and making its sole purpose the serving of our appetites.

What is needed is repentance. In order of priority, I think that first we should repent of our sins against God (Psalms 32, 38, 51). Then there should be repentance for our sins against others. And then I believe we should repent of those sins we have committed against the environment.

It would not be a bad idea for us to set aside a day once a year to confess our sins of environmental terrorism. It would be good for us to periodically acknowledge that because of sins against the environment, we have limited nature's power to magnify and worship the Lord. We have so altered nature, as we have selfishly exploited it, that glory is now being deflected from God. We have hurt nature in an obscene effort to satiate our egoism, and we have dishonored our God. Surely, repentance is in order. Part of our priestly calling as Christians is to lead the peoples of the earth into repentance before our God and to call upon the people to change their ways.

If we acknowledge that all of creation was meant to worship and glorify God, then we simultaneously sense that we are called to rescue creation so that it can fulfill this calling. To commit ourselves to creation-care is to commit ourselves to releasing creation from its distortions so that it can join us in worship. To clean up the environment, to work for the renewal of all species (as we have done for the whales), and to plant trees is to add to the chorus of voices that praise the Lord.

The ecological movement must not be understood solely in terms of human welfare. The call to beautify and maintain the environment must not be viewed only as a call to serve our own self-interests.

At the core of what we do to rescue a growing creation from the abuses of people should be a deep commitment to free nature to join us in the worship of God. Our efforts for creation-care should come out of a desire to bring all of creation to the throne of grace in order to sing His praises and to declare His goodness. These spiritual kinds of concerns and motivations are what distinguish us from those other social action groups that do not claim to be based on biblical imperatives. This understanding of creation-care as a Christian mission is what makes involvement in the ecological movement a Christian vocation.

Hymn writers William M. Ruyan and T. O. Chisholm understood that our relationship to nature should be full of revelation and worship when they gave us the great hymn "Great Is Thy Faithfulness," which inspires us with these words:

> Summer and winter,
> And springtime and harvest,
> Sun, moon, and stars
> In their courses above,
> Join with all nature
> In manifold witness
> To Thy great faithfulness,
> Mercy, and love.[1]

11

THE GREENING
OF THE CHURCH

Getting the Church Involved
in Environmental Concerns

I believe that the church is the "now" body of Christ.
Two thousand years ago, the eternal Christ incarnated
Himself in Jesus of Nazareth. In that mortal body, Christ
spoke and acted in the midst of our world; He did His
Father's will on earth.

In today's world, the body of Christ is the church.
Through the church, God's contemporary work on earth
is accomplished. The eternal Christ chooses to speak to
our world through the church. And if this world is to
hear God's message about creation-care, it will be
through the church.

There is a tendency among Christians bent on addressing the pressing issues of our day to discount the importance of the church and even to write off those small bodies of believers who meet in a hundred thousand buildings of various shapes and sizes across America. Yet those people in those varied gatherings, with all of their shortcomings and pettiness, are still an incarnation of the eternal Christ. God has given them the awesome task of calling the world to repentance for all of its sins, including the sins against creation. He has given the church the task of showing the world His design for life and happiness.

MOBILIZING LOCAL CONGREGATIONS

With respect to the concerns about the environment, the church has done very little to speak to the world about God and to make known His will. Time is short, and the church must act quickly to make up for its failures of the past. I've already suggested some of the things it ought to say about creation-care, but here are some specific things local congregations can do to help save the environment.

Give to Development Ministries That Are Ecologically Conscious

Time and time again I hear from those who run Christian relief organizations that the only way they can get financial support from individual donors is by promoting child sponsorships. The appeals via magazine ads and TV specials that show the sad eyes and emaciated bodies of malnourished Third World children are a sure way to get people to make monthly pledges.

I head a missionary relief organization that has made a transition from a child support system that provided care for individual boys and girls to a system that provides ecologically sound development programs. Whereas we once spent twenty dollars a month to take care of a specific child in a Third World country, the Evangelical Association for the Promotion of Education (E.A.P.E.) now asks its sponsors to contribute the same amount of money in the same regular fashion for development projects. These projects benefit and bless all the children of a given village, not just the one child whom the sponsor supports.[1]

Consequently, E.A.P.E. has been able to use the money donated to develop such things as tree-planting programs, irrigation systems, and wells. Over the past few years, we who are with E.A.P.E. have worked hard to create cottage industries. These small industries are now providing employment alternatives to the "slash and burn" farming that has been destroying the forests and leading to massive soil erosion in poor countries.

The transition that moved E.A.P.E. into ecologically responsible development projects came as a result not so much of thoughtful reflection, but rather of emotional reactions experienced on the field.

In the past, when our missionaries visited the communities where our sponsored children lived, they were very upset by seeing what was happening to the children who were not part of our sponsorship program. One of our missionaries let me know of her distress in no uncertain terms:

> You could not go on with this child support program if you could see what really happens in the villages.

The sponsored kids go to school while the others who are left out of the program stand at the windows of the school looking in. The sponsored kids get clothes, and at Christmas they get toys while the others get nothing. Yes, there even are times when the kids we support get to eat while the others go hungry.

What could I say? I knew we had to change things so that we could testify to a God who does not have favorites and who loves each and every child with His infinite love. Thus, we shifted to community development programs.

When we told our child support sponsors the reasons for the shift, we received very wide support. Granted, there were a handful of sponsors who objected to this new way of doing things, but we were able to refer them to other organizations that have more traditional child support programs. After the change was made, we found that well over 95 percent of our sponsors had shifted to the new system and had done so with a good understanding and an appreciation of what we were trying to do. Their encouragement and continued giving has provided the support we need to do missionary work in ways that show a deep concern for the environment while still expressing love for the hurting, desperately poor children whom we had previously helped.

At E.A.P.E., we not only desire donations but are even more interested in recruits. We need ecologically conscious missionaries who can take to the field not only a deep commitment to declaring the personal salvation wrought in Christ, but who will also bring a message of justice which includes the rescuing of creation from its troubled and polluted state. We need missionaries ready to make known the good news that our God is at work not only to make people new but also to make all the rest of His creation new too.

I, myself, have been a strong promoter of child support programs, and through my speaking engagements, I have enlisted more than ten thousand child sponsors. Through organizations such as World Vision and Compassion International, twenty dollars a month will provide holistic care for a child in a Third World country. That means that for seventy cents a day (that's less than you pay for a cup of coffee), you can feed, clothe, educate, and evangelize a needy child in some desperate setting like Zaire or Vietnam.

However, as essential and caring as such child sponsorship programs are, they do little to solve the long-term problems of poverty and hunger that plague people in the economically oppressed countries of the world. Those who lead Christian relief organizations are the first to admit that fact. These leaders very much want to invest financial and human resources in development programs that will increase the availability of food. But it is hard to get people to designate gifts for such causes. Asking people to make monthly gifts for digging wells, buying fertilizers, or building irrigation trenches lacks the emotional appeal of the face of a pleading child. Leaders of Christian relief organizations would be more than willing to do more development work if they just had the money to do it.

What you can do is let the relief agency of your choice know that you want to make an ongoing monthly commitment for development work. But be even more specific. State your desire to support the kind of development programs that are ecologically responsible. Tell of your desire to see more programs which work toward the reforestation of land that has been devastated by "slash and burn" farming. Express your interest in efforts that would curtail the growth of deserts in regions like the Sahel of Africa. Let relief organizations know that you want to support programs that endorse controlling population growth. Your requests and inquiries will encourage them to pursue developmental solutions to poverty. And by raising ecological concerns, you will motivate them to pursue programs that can restore the land to a state of beauty, health, and *shalom*.

World Vision and Compassion International are sensitive and committed to development, but they need more encouragement to incorporate ecologically sound practices into their programs. Support them and prod them toward greater responsibility for the environment.[2]

Start a Christian "ReLeaf" Campaign

An option that is particularly important for Christians who live in urban areas is to organize ecologically conscious church members into tree planting campaigns. The big cities of America are, for the most part, on the verge of bankruptcy. As these cities cut their spending, one of the first things to go is any ongoing program to plant trees. "But trees are a fundamental building block of a healthy urban environment," says Dan Smith of the American Forestry Association. "Planting trees is one of the most cost-effective ways to attack carbon dioxide buildup in the atmosphere."[3]

Tree shade can save up to 40 percent on air conditioning costs, and the protection that trees provide against winter winds can cut our heating bills by 10 percent or more. This does not even take into account the aesthetic contribution they make to city life!

The fact is that 45 percent of the cities of America do not have a tree-planting program, and those cities that do have drastically cut back these programs.

But Christians can strike back. They can organize church members into "ReLeaf Teams" and arrange with their respective cities to plant trees. This kind of tree planting is a whole new kind of missionary work for urban Christians. It becomes a way for the church to say "we care" to the rest of the community and for Christians to live out their calling to rescue dying creation. Planting new life is a declaration of the gospel.

There are many private groups outside the church that are already engaged in ReLeaf programs. In Tucson, Arizona, five thousand residents formed a ReLeaf group that has planted over one hundred and fifty thousand trees in the last two years. In Houston, a team of twenty-five citizens plant up to three thousand trees annually. And in my own city of Philadelphia, a citizen's group plants more than three hundred mature trees each year.

Starting a ReLeaf campaign can be a perfect program for a church youth group or for the men's fellowship and/or women's missionary society. Such a campaign can make the church very visible as a viable part of the ecology movement and can elicit much gratitude from the community. But more importantly, a church-sponsored ReLeaf program can send a message to those outside the church that our God is a God who works through people to renew His world. It can be one more sign to the world that our God is a God whose salvation is *for this world* and not just an escape to the next one.

Teach the Church to Love Animals

I am always a bit surprised when I realize that seldom, if ever, is there any mention of animal care in Sunday school lessons. Churches rarely provide the kind of teachings that would help children (and adults, for that matter) understand what God requires of them as far as caring for animals. If nothing else, don't ministers and priests realize that cruel adult behavior often has its beginnings in a child's torturing of a cat? Why do they not make it clear that God has compassion for animals as well as for humans (Jonah 4:11)?

I was pleasantly surprised during a visit to New York City when I happened upon a special day of blessings for animals at the great Cathedral of St. John the Divine. Once a year, a Sunday afternoon is designated for people to bring their animals to this Episcopal church in order to receive blessings and prayers from the pastors. All kinds of people bring all kinds of animals so that the clergy might lay hands on these special creatures in the name of Christ. What made this service particularly amazing to me was that, in addition to an array of the expected house pets, a variety of New York Zoo animals, ranging from a camel to sheep and goats, were on hand to be blessed. Some tourists visiting the church that afternoon were amused. But others, perhaps for the first time in their lives, considered the special place that animals hold in God's scheme of things.

This unusual church service was a brilliant educational tool. I since have found Anglican churches both in the United States and in the United Kingdom that regularly observe the ministry of blessing the animals. Roman Catholics also carry on this practice. Other denominations should pick up this idea and make it a regular part of church life. We must explore all ways to raise the awareness of church people to the reality that animals have a right to a blessed life and have a uniquely ordained role to play in worshiping God that stands apart from any utilitarian function they perform for us humans.

DO AN ENVIRONMENTAL AUDIT AT CHURCH

Tim Cooper, an intensely evangelical British Christian who is also a leader in the green party of the United Kingdom, advocates that each church regularly audit itself to determine the extent of its commitment to being ecologically responsible. Among the questions he suggests that each congregation ask itself are:[4]

- Are church newsletters and stationery printed on recycled paper?
- Is waste recycled whenever appropriate?
- Is the church using reusable cups, plates, and cutlery for socials and dinners?
- Is the choice of food served at church functions influenced by considerations such as global poverty and the kind of factory farming that forces animals to suffer?
- Are other materials, such as cleaning products, environmentally safe?
- If the church has financial investments or an endowment, are the funds in an institution or account that is ecologically responsible?[5]
- Are the church buildings used efficiently, and are they properly insulated? To maintain a building that is used only an hour or two a week is wasteful and represents poor stewardship. A congregation should ask itself if its buildings could be used during weekdays.

OTHER MOBILIZATION IDEAS

Recycle Sales

If the church has garage sales or rummage sales, it should rename them "recycle sales." This is a chance to testify to the rest of the community that Christianity is an alternative to the throw-away life-style that has become a hallmark of our times.

Better still, the church could set up a thrift shop, more appropriately named a "recycle shop." A room, easily accessible to people who might come off the street, could be open daily. Staffed by church volunteers, especially by those who are retired, this shop could establish itself as a place where people throughout the community could bring a variety of things—good clothing, household appliances, furniture, and all sorts of bric-a-brac—for resale.

Poor people in the community will consider such a recycle shop a godsend. But even the church's more affluent neighbors will appreciate this kind of store. The recycle shop can be part of the message that the Christian life-style requires refraining from unnecessary expensive buying and promotes a spending pattern that is responsible to others. In this way, the financial resources that God has placed in our hands can be used more fully and directly to do His work.

Redefine Stewardship Sunday

Almost every church has a stewardship Sunday. And almost every pastor knows that if the church is going to have enough money to keep going, it has to challenge its people to pledge financial support. But we should broaden the concept of *stewardship* from simply filling out pledge cards, which designate weekly financial contributions to ongoing church programs, to a commitment to a socially responsible life-style.

Those churches which have a tradition of giving "invitations" should consider inviting their members to come to the altar on stewardship Sunday as a way of making a public declaration of their willingness to live lives that express social justice and ecological stewardship. Too often those in the pews are reduced to being passive listeners instead of being called upon to do something about the things that they have heard from the pulpit. People must be challenged to make decisions, especially about their personal life-style.

What is involved in being a disciple of Christ should be discussed with the congregation and not simply dictated by the clergy. The people of God must be of one accord when deciding what constitutes a biblically prescribed life-style (Acts 1:14, 2:1, 2:46, 12:20, 15:25). But in the end, we should not be reluctant to call people to publicly declare what they are willing to do and be. And ecological responsibility should be part of that commitment.

In this context, stewardship Sunday could and should be lifted to a higher level of understanding. It should be a day when time and resources are yielded up to God by the people of the church. And it also should be a day in which commitments are made to care for the creation that God has placed in our hands.

Speak to the "Larger Body of Christ"

Each local church congregation should recognize that it is only a local manifestation of that larger body of believers called in Scripture the "body of Christ." All Christians everywhere are connected to each other through the Holy Spirit who makes us one. Each local church has a responsibility to edify other congregations in the body of Christ.

Churches that have become aware of the biblical imperative to be good caretakers must be ready to communicate ecological responsibility to other congregations as they share with one another what God has revealed. One way to do this is through proposing resolutions at denominational gatherings, calling Christendom to ecological responsibility. All the mainline denominations have regular conclaves that bring together representatives of local congregations in order to handle church business and to establish denominational policy. As part of these gatherings, there are always times when contemporary social and moral issues are discussed and resolutions passed. If God has spoken to a particular church about caring for His creation, it is a good idea for representatives of that ecologically conscious local congregation to use such opportunities to sensitize other congregations to crucial environmental concerns.

Most religious gatherings of this kind are more than willing to pass resolutions that address environmental concerns in a general way. Problems arise when members demand specific actions.

To some, it may seem ludicrous to propose a resolution that member churches of a particular denomination not use styrofoam cups for coffee at church functions. Such a motion may seem trivial in the context of awesome concerns for world evangelism, feeding the hungry, and nuclear disarmament. It helps, when possible, to have resolutions related to some pending government legislation such as controls on automobile emissions or a "pure water" act. But only by addressing these "little" concerns one by one can we change the overall condition of our planet.

Resolutions must be specific. Everybody supports a clean environment in principle. Opposition only surfaces when cleaning up the environment costs money or creates inconvenience. That is why we Christians must declare loud and clear that we are willing to pay the price and endure the stresses that go with creation-care. Faithfulness to Christ requires that we do nothing less. Jesus told us that if we are faithful in the little things, He will make us rulers over great things (Matthew 25:21).

Even if your church does not belong to a denomination, it probably is related to some kind of corporate Christian fellowship such as the National Association of Evangelicals or the Evangelical Alliance. Resolutions on ecological issues at such gatherings would have a powerful effect.

Use the Church Grounds as a Recycle Center

Finding a location for a recycling center where people in the community can deposit used cans, bottles, and paper can be difficult. Since the bins are often considered eyesores, few neighborhoods want them in their backyards.

Enter the church!

The local church can demonstrate its calling to servant ministry by having these bins displayed prominently on church property. Advertise to the rest of the community about the link between recycling and the biblically prescribed mandate not to waste God's resources and clutter His creation.

The signs might read:

**God Wants To Turn
our Trash into Something Good!**

The God of Creation Is
Also the God of Recreation—Recycle
Our God Makes Everything New Again

These bins can serve as a constant reminder that the church considers itself God's agent for cleaning up and maintaining the environment.

Church families could deposit their recyclable items on Sundays as they come to worship, thus teaching everyone, especially children, that ecological conservation is part of what it means to be Christian.

There is one more good thing that can come from all of this. Money can be made from recycling. Used bottles, aluminum cans, and old newspapers can be sold, and the dollars they bring in can be used for a variety of good things. My suggestion is that the profits from recycling be set aside for ministries to the poor. By using the money for such purposes as shelter for the homeless, care for the elderly, and soup kitchens for street people, the witness of the church to the community is lifted to an even higher level.

Sponsor Ecological Work Camps

The kind of activities that church youth groups sponsor has changed over the years. When I was a teenager, the big thing was to go away to camp. Every denomination responded to that interest by establishing church camps and investing heavily in camping programs. The benefit that denominations gained through camping was enormous. A significant proportion of all commitments to Christ and the church were made at camps. Camping proved to be a primary means for recruiting young people for the pastoral ministry and for missionary service.

Most of us who attended church camp will attest to the emotional and spiritual impact that camping experiences can have. Standing in a circle around a campfire, singing "Kum-ba-Yah" may seem a bit corny in retrospect, but at the time what happened to us was probably very significant. I personally can attest to the importance of Christian camping, and I would even go so far as to say that without the experiences I had at camp, I am not sure if my commitment to Christ would have ever been firmly established.

But camping has become passé. Teenagers today have so many broadening experiences and travel so widely that, to most of them, camping is a drag. It takes much more than going to church camp to excite them.

Increasingly, youth leaders have looked for alternatives to the typical summer camping experience. One of those options has been youth mission trips. Organizing young people into "work groups," youth leaders have been taking teenagers to places like Haiti and Mexico to serve and be with the poor. These work groups have built schools, churches, and housing for the poor. They have worked amazingly hard and at great sacrifice to serve people in Third World countries. Their contributions have been significant, while they themselves have been sensitized to the plight of the poor and have been challenged to work for justice on behalf of the oppressed.

The mission organization that I serve, the Evangelical Association for the Promotion of Education, is structured to handle scores of these work groups each year. I personally have seen the impact that being a part of a work group can make on the life of a young person. I have witnessed what I sometimes call a "second conversion" as teenagers reevaluate their lives while they live among the poor in a missionary situation.

There is a particular kind of missions work camp for teenagers that could make a significant contribution toward the greening of the church—an environmental work camp. The youth leader could organize teenagers of the church to clean up and restore a beachfront or pond. A park area might be the target. In many cities, funds for the care of parks and recreation areas are inadequate. A church work group could respond by cleaning such a place.

The group could use a church located close to the work site as a place to eat and sleep. They could spend their days cleaning up the targeted area, making sure to appropriately separate collected trash so that it can be recycled. They could spend some time each evening studying and reflecting on the consequences of pollution, the significance of their own labors, and what the Bible has to say about it all.

When the young people return to their home church, give them the opportunity to share and interpret their experiences to the rest of the congregation at a special evening service. That way, the work group could broaden the understanding of the rest of the congregation about environmental issues.

Provide Constant Reminders

Keeping the congregation aware of environmental concerns is an ongoing task. A special committee of those who are especially concerned about these matters should be appointed and given the task of holding their concerns before the church. Among the things that they might do is use the front and back of church bulletins to tell their story. Most denominational presses already have developed folders for church bulletins with pictures, scriptures, and written statements to prompt parishioners to be environmentally sensitive. By contacting bookstores of various denominations, you can secure a variety of these folders. The committee should not hesitate to make its own church bulletins. The Sunday morning crowd will appreciate seeing the creativity of its own members. Furthermore, this is an opportunity to let some church members who have artistic skills use their gifts in Christian service.

Even if the entire church bulletin is not designated to heighten environmental awareness, there can be a small notice in each weekly bulletin. In weekly notices, the committee could suggest things that members could do to be environmentally responsible. There are many books available on the care of the environment that could provide specific suggestions.

The committee could prepare and hang in the church sanctuary banners which herald environmental concerns. Once again, those in the church who have artistic gifts can be called on to make significant contributions. The banners could say:

Live Simply That Others
Might Simply Live

Be Good Stewards
of God's Creation

Enjoy but Don't Destroy
What God Has Created

These colorful banners can be constant reminders to those who worship that creation-care is part of being a Christian.

Include hymns about creation and the care of the environment in worship. Surveying the hymnals presently being used for church worship will provide an array of hymns about the environment that are too often ignored.

Many familiar hymns have messages about appreciating God through nature and encourage us to recognize the sacred character of creation. Examples of such hymns are: "O Lord, Our Lord, in All the Earth," "All Creatures of Our God and King," "This is My Father's World," "God Who Touchest Earth with Beauty," and "The Spacious Firmament on High."

Hymns are great teaching tools. Sometimes I think that the theological thinking of people in churches is more conditioned by the hymns they sing than by the sermons they hear. I know that in my own church, which is an African-American congregation, the preacher often validates a point he is making by quoting from a hymn. The people in the congregation will surely resonate to what the preacher is saying when his message is supported by the recitation of a hymn that has long been part of their lives. Hymns as vehicles for truth should not be underestimated. Use hymns to tell the story of God's love for His creation.

Make Creation-Care Part of Discipling

Most churches require potential members to undergo a training period, usually through some kind of discipleship class. Here, would-be new members learn what the church believes and what is expected of them as members. These classes provide an ideal opportunity to sensitize Christians to their responsibilities to care for the environment and to respect the lives of all God's creatures. The pastor, or whoever else is teaching the class, might secure written and audio visual materials that will tell the story of how all of this fits into the Christian lifestyle. The Mennonites have provided some excellent material for just this purpose in *Whole People Whole Earth: Shalom Lifestyles*, by Jerry L. Holsopple (Harrisonburg, VA: Mennonite Media Productions).

We must make it clear to those who come into the church that being a Christian is much more than just giving intellectual assent to propositional truths. We need to let them know that it involves even more than living lives of personal holiness and spiritual purity. We must help them to understand that being a Christian requires a commitment to social justice. In that context, ample time and teaching should be given to environmental concerns.

Tell new members that responsible Christians drive cars that create minimal pollution and that they also refrain from driving as much as possible. Encourage them to see that refusal to buy products like deodorants or insect sprays in aerosol cans is a Christian obligation. As Christians they ought to know that certain detergents and throw-away diapers are ecologically sinful. In short, they must be introduced to forms of sin and righteousness that will seem, in all probability, completely new and somewhat strange to them.

It must be recognized that in the end the evils that have befallen the environment, primarily at the hands of those who live in industrially developed nations, will only be eliminated as individuals opt for a new, responsible, Christian life-style. The church must demonstrate not only to its own members but to those outside the church just what this new life-style is all about. Over and against the selfish consumerism that is the hallmark of our times should stand Christians who bear witness to their Lord by living lives of responsible nonconformity. What we Christians buy, what we use, and what we throw away should demonstrate that we care about God's world. New church members must see that Christian living requires that we go far beyond the simple pieties of the past. They must learn that being Christian determines all that they say and do.

This is only the beginning of the list of things that churches can do to develop environmentally responsible members. There is one church I know that has a service each year in a local park so that people can experience the joys and preciousness of nature while they worship. I know of another church that has painted its doors green and posted plaques on them explaining that the green doors are to remind all who enter that they are to keep God's creation green and beautiful.

Such exercises might seem trivial to some and relatively small to others. But we must remember that our Lord emphatically taught us that faithfulness in such little things is what changes things on the macro level.

Let Judgment Begin with the House of God

Local churches must be role models of biblically prescribed discipleship in relationship to the environment. Sooner or later the rest of the world will wake up to the urgency which the impending ecological disaster poses, and when that day comes, they will embrace a host of corrective programs. The church must be in the forefront with the initiatives and leadership that offer them hope.

We must be in the forefront of the green movement. The green movement gives us an opportunity to show that the salvation which comes in Christ is more than just a provision to escape hell and get into heaven when we die. It is a chance to illustrate that not only is our God committed to making *us* into "new" creatures, but also He is committed to the renewal of all creation and to bringing justice to bear in all our relationships.

We have, through our participation in the movement to save the environment, an opportunity to witness to the relevance of God's salvation to all of life. The willingness of people to consider Christ as Savior is, in fact, related to their perception of Christ as the hope of the world in the face of what otherwise would be a dismal future. If nothing else, involvement in the green movement will put us into intensive dialogue with a host of people—who would otherwise be unwilling to talk to Christians—about how our biblical faith influences the world in which we live.

If we in the church do not act, other religious groups, such as the New Age movement, will step in and usurp a cause to which God has called us. We know that the New Agers have already become identified with the call to ecological salvation. Their talk of "Mother Earth" and their theology of *Gaia* have become part of the dialogue on environmental concerns. We cannot let those who embrace a pagan religion take charge of a movement that will be a major concern of most enlightened people for the next couple of decades.

Christians must set the agenda. We are the people who must declare the salvation of God for the cosmos. The church must lead the way for ecological renewal. God has commissioned His people to be the agents through whom He rescues this world from its polluted condition (Romans 8:19–23). Let us be faithful.

12

Changing the World with a Majority of One

Focusing on Individual Responsibility

I once saw a cartoon that depicted a huge mass of people. The crowd stretched as far as the eye could see. Over each person was one of those balloons that cartoonists use. In this cartoon, each person in the gigantic crowd was saying, "What can one person do?"

Perhaps the most evil thing any of us can do in the face of the immense environmental problem that confronts us is to give up. When any one person stops to consider all that has gone wrong with humanity's stewardship of God's creation, it seems almost justifiable to throw up one's hands and ask, "What's the use?"

Such resignation is not allowed for followers of Christ. As the Holy Spirit gains control in the life of a Christian, there comes a still, small voice that whispers, "You can make a difference."

When it comes to environmental concerns, we must strongly affirm the significance of the individual. God saved you and expects you to act as His agent here on earth. He is calling upon *you* to do what *you* can do to deliver nature from its suffering and to prevent the destruction of the atmosphere.

STARTING WITH THE ANIMALS

To be a Christian is to be kind to animals. We all know that kindness is required by God in our relationships with each other, but few seem to realize that the Bible makes clear that God declares cruelty to animals to be sin (Proverbs 12:10). As Christians opposed to sin in any and all forms, we ought to consider fulfilling our obligation to nature by delivering animals, in so far as it is possible, from suffering and unnecessary death.

Every Christian home should be "cruelty free." It appalls me that parents so often allow their children to mistreat animals. At zoos, I have seen parents stand idly by while their children torment animals in cages. At the beach, I have watched children chase after sea gulls with no other purpose than to scare them. And I have visited homes where animals were nothing more than toys for the children, who were free to mistreat them as they saw fit.

Don't these parents know that these attitudes can pattern their children into a hardness and meanness that is contrary to the will of God? Don't they sense the damage to their testimony as caring Christians?

Christians can teach their children that kindness can be shown when we give a guard dog a place to run and play, when we stop to give a carriage horse a drink of water, and when we care enough to help a lost animal return to his or her home. If you do not think that such simple acts of kindness give to children a taste of godliness, then your God is too small.

We *must* teach children tenderness toward animals because, for children, animals are usually the only creatures more vulnerable and helpless than themselves. Children learn how to treat those who have less power than they do as they relate to these innocent creatures of God.

Once when I took my children to the zoo, my daughter Lisa let me know that she did not enjoy it. She told me that she thought it was wrong to put animals in cages just so we could see them. The more I think about what she said, the more I think she was right.

Julia Allen Field once wrote, "We cannot glimpse the essential life of a caged animal, only the shadow of her former beauty."

Zoos, I suppose, serve some good purposes. There are certain species of animals that would be extinct if zoos did not provide them with a protected environment. But there is something about animals in cages that seems to fly in the face of what I believe to be the will of God. You may deem me a bit ridiculous, but with Emile Zola, I must say, "The fate of animals is of greater importance to me than the fear of appearing ridiculous; it is indissolubly connected with the fate of men."

Birds in cages particularly make me sad. To have creatures that were created to soar in the sky boxed in behind wires seems all wrong to me. William Blake, in *Inquiries of Innocence*, wrote, "A robin red breast in a cage / Puts all Heaven in a rage."

I believe that, in this respect, Blake knew more about the hosts of heaven than do a lot of Christian theologians.

If zoos must exist, those who build them should create conditions that approximate the natural habitat as much as possible. I saw such a setting for gorillas in the Atlanta Zoo. And the wonderful zoo in Singapore gives animals such a natural place to live that the place does not seem to be a zoo at all. It may seem a bit odd to say, but when I left the Singapore Zoo, I had the feeling of having just visited some happy friends.

In California, the San Diego Zoo has created a huge animal preserve just north of the city. Visitors ride through the wild animal park on a monorail train, and what they see is a far cry from the sight of caged animals that we find in typical zoos. Whole herds roam over miles of open space.

Beverly Armstrong writes in *The Animal Voice:*

> How would you like to live in a cage that is just about ten feet square with no toy to play with and nothing to do—just you and a bed and a chair? You'd get mad and scream and throw things around. You'd kick and you'd paint on the wall, and your owners would scold you, and say to themselves, "He isn't a nice pet at all!"[1]

I also have a problem with Sea World and other such centers of entertainment that put dolphins and whales into restrictive tanks. What confinement does to dolphins who navigate by sonar is hard to imagine. Dolphins and whales get so depressed in captivity that most of them won't breed. In the ocean dolphins travel thirty-five miles per hour and cover forty miles a day. At Sea World, sixteen of them share with two beluga whales a tank that is eighty feet long and thirteen feet deep. Do you think that God cares?

Another thing that gets to me are the all too common "puppy mills." We do not need them. Animal shelters in communities from one end of this country to the other are bursting with unwanted animals. Anybody who wants a dog can go and rescue one of them from death. In spite of that fact, over three hundred thousand puppies are bred in puppy mill kennels where "farmers" turn them out for sale at pet stores. In these kennels, female dogs are bred continuously, with no rest between cycles. And when their bodies wear out, they are killed.

Almost 25 percent of federally licensed breeding kennels operate under substandard conditions, according to the U.S. Department of Agriculture. The dogs in these kennels, for the most part, live in cramped and filthy conditions. Buying dogs from pet shops often means you are contributing to this obscene cruelty.

Animals are blessings. They are fun and helpful. Playing with a cat can generate childlike joy, and a good dog can give more peace of mind than a burglar alarm. Watching the birds eat the crumbs we throw out in the back yard can provide hours of fascination. Spending time observing fish in a home aquarium can soothe our nerves after an upsetting day (there are scientific studies to support this claim). Animals can provide us with spiritual comfort.

After enduring forty days in the wilderness and the powerful temptations of Satan, Jesus found renewal with angels and animals, according to Scripture (Mark 1:13).

We must recognize that God uses animals sacramentally as a means of grace. They are one means for restoring our souls and granting us the heavenly Father's benediction.

In a study done at the University of Texas, researchers discovered that when elderly people receive animals to stroke and pet, the aging process and the onset of senility slows down. At the University of Pennsylvania, social scientists are discovering that sociopathic children who are given animals to care for and to call their own gradually become responsible, caring persons.

I personally witnessed dogs effectively used to help children with stuttering problems overcome their speech impediments. When small children relate to dogs, they tend to talk to them as though the animals were siblings. With children who have difficulty in forming words and speaking, communicating with animals provides excellent speech therapy. A child with speech problems that are not physiologically based can often learn to speak in a relatively normal manner when talking to his or her dog. If the child is encouraged to carry on lengthy "conversations" with the dog, this practice tends to reduce or eliminate the stuttering in his or her conversations with other people.

Perhaps because it doesn't talk back, the dog is nonthreatening to the child, and in the relaxed conditions that go with being in the company of a beloved pet, many psychological barriers to a normal speech pattern evaporate. The relationship with the dog provides the child with the kind of self-confidence necessary for normal conversations with others. Talking to animals evidently provides good training for talking with people.

Dogs and cats provide companionship and offer unconditional love and acceptance for those who otherwise might feel lonely and rejected. We are sometimes amazed at the depth of feeling that people can have for the animals who fill their emotional needs.

Near my home, there is a cemetery for small animals. I love to take friends who visit me to see that cemetery. The grass is neatly trimmed, and more often than not, there are cut flowers on some of the graves. Once, while talking to the caretaker of the cemetery, I observed an elderly woman reverently meditating beside a tombstone that read "Kelly—My Best Friend." When the caretaker told me that she was a widow, I jokingly asked, "I wonder if she is that thoughtful of her dead husband."

"Probably not," he answered. "But then if you had known both her husband and her dog, you would more than understand."

Such are the blessings of animals. No wonder God ordered Noah to save them from the great Flood.

But we humans have been irresponsible in our husbandry of animals. We have neglected them and abused them. Pets often endure undeserved suffering at the hands of their owners.

At Christmas and Easter, young children often receive pets to enjoy without any supervision or guidance. In most cases, the children do not receive any sense that the animals are a sacred trust from God and that God holds them and their parents responsible for what happens to these precious creatures. It is an ugly thing to see an unsupervised child hurting an animal "just for fun." What is even worse is when parents are on hand and ignore the cruelty.

The final tragedy is when they abandon their pets because the children tire of them or the parents think them inconvenient to keep. There are those who, before going on summer vacation, take the dog or cat, which had been a Christmas present, and drop it off in some deserted spot to fend for itself. With no thought about the painful confusion and hunger their one-time pet may have to endure, they drive off, unaware that God is not indifferent to what they have done. Don't they realize that God gave them the responsibility for those animals they adopted into their families?

THE LAND IS THE LORD'S

Personal responsibility for the land is also part of being a Christian. The Scriptures state that land belongs to the Lord and not to those who usually claim to own it. I say "usually" because in many places in the world, land is never considered private property. For most of human history, the majority of cultures believed that the land belonged to God and had been given to them as a sacred trust to use with care and charity.

The Scriptures pick up that same theme (Psalm 24:1–2; 1 Corinthians 10:26). Because the land is the Lord's, we are to treat it with loving care and not exploit it. Those in the early church who lived in Jerusalem shared their land with each other and treated it as a gift from God (Acts 4:32–35). Furthermore, we find in the Old Testament an underpreached commandment of God to live *sabbatically:*

> Six years you shalt sow your field, and six years you shall prune your vineyard, and gather in its fruit; but in the seventh year there shall be a sabbath of solemn rest for the land, a sabbath to the LORD. You shall neither sow your field nor prune your vineyard. What grows of its own accord of your harvest you shall not reap, nor gather the grapes of your untended vine, for it is a year of rest for the land. (Leviticus 25:3–5)

Here God commands that we nurture the land, give it time for renewal, and treat it as a holy trust. In this passage, He calls upon us to exercise the kind of creation-care that has been the theme of this book. In today's world, here are some practical ways to obey this commandment.

Be Sure Your Lawn Is Safe

Lawn care has become a major factor in the dismal ecological conditions which pose such a threat to our future. The vast array of chemical weed killers that are now being used on lawns across America are a source of water pollution and a threat to our health. These chemicals are often washed into streams and rivers. They seep into wells. They end up threatening fish and other forms of pond life. Often household pets are poisoned by these chemicals. Even worse, chemical poisoning from the weed killers may become a threat to the health of small children who play on the lawn. In addition to the significant pollution, the chemical fertilizers require an exorbitant amount of a limited water supply that we can ill afford to waste.

We may need to conclude that the green lawns which have become a hallmark of our suburban life-style are something we cannot responsibly include in our future.

Save Water in the Name of Jesus

We are running out of fresh, clean water. As the population of the world explodes, the shortage of usable drinking water may prove to be a more serious problem than the more apparent shortage of food. A significant proportion of the water supply in Third World countries is polluted. This contaminated water is undoubtedly the major cause of dysentery and may be the dominant factor influencing high infant mortality rates in these countries. Furthermore, there is such a shortage of any kind of water in the Third World that even this polluted water is in short supply.

In Africa, I have personally seen armed guards positioned to keep thirsty nomads from getting water out of depleted reservoirs. In Haiti, I have seen beggars plead, not for money or food, but for fresh water.

But the shortage of fresh water is not just a Third World problem. Here in the United States, we have begun to feel the impact of the scarcity of decent drinking water. Between pollution and overpopulation, we are witnessing a diminished availability of water, particularly in our concentrated urban areas. Wherever there is any kind of drought in places like New York or Los Angeles, we can count on local government authorities to enact water restrictions. Can the rationing of water be far off?

Also, the quality of the water we are drinking has become a major concern among those in charge of public health. There are children in some communities in the United States who are mentally retarded because of high levels of lead in their drinking water. And cancer-causing elements at dangerous levels are commonly discovered in the water that comes from the faucets in our own homes. Because of water contamination, much of the fish we eat contains dangerous amounts of mercury.

Such alarming facts require immediate action. All of us must learn to conserve water and to recognize that the stewardship of this essential natural resource is part of Christian discipleship. Our responsibility as caretakers of God's creation, as well as our responsibility to others in His name, requires that we be committed to doing a host of simple things day in and day out which will insure enough good water for everyone. The following is a partial list of the things that we should commit to do:

- Place a rock in every water tank attached to every toilet in your home. Don't use a brick; it can break apart and clog your system. You will save hundreds of gallons per month.

- Take short showers. Install a low-flow shower head, which will save the average household three to four thousand gallons of water per person each year.

- Check your faucets. One drop per second wastes more than twenty-four thousand gallons per year.

- Avoid the use of nonbiodegradable detergents when doing the wash.

- Do not run your dishwasher or washing machine unless you have a full load.

- Make sure that there are good washers on all the faucets in your home.

- (I like this one!) Wash your car as seldom as possible. Do not insist on a spotless car.

Remember That Christians Buy Green

The marketplace is by no means a democracy. A minority of buyers can disproportionately influence what is sold and how it is sold. Consumers are becoming sensitized to the environmental damage caused by the things they buy and the packaging used in preparing products for sale. And as consumers publicize their concerns about the environment, those in the marketplace have responded rapidly. Buyers can make a difference.

In 1989, marketing researchers with the Michael Peters Group discovered that one-half of all consumers during the previous year had chosen not to buy a product if they believed that either it or the packaging might be harmful to the environment. They also found that 61 percent of the consumers interviewed said that they would be more inclined to patronize a store that showed signs of concern over the environment. Those who sell in the world's marketplace are becoming increasingly aware of the environmental concerns of their buyers, and before long, we will see major changes in what is being sold and how it is packaged for sale.[2]

Another hopeful discovery made by the research of the Michael Peters Group is that consumers are willing to pay 5 percent more for products packaged with recyclable or biodegradable materials. That is really good news because it demonstrates the willingness of consumers to overcome pure selfishness and buy with concern for others in mind. Creation-care is going to hit us in the pocketbook, and it is good to know that consumers are ready and willing for that to happen.[3]

Environmental concern expressed in the buying preferences of consumers is even getting huge multinational corporations to take notice. Wal-Mart, a national discount store chain, ran full-page ads in the newspapers, challenging its suppliers to provide products packaged in ways that are environmentally sound. Proctor and Gamble, one of the biggest companies in the country, received so much criticism about the pollution caused by Pampers that it is trying out a recycling program to see if the problems created by Pampers can be resolved. Cascade-Dominion, a Canadian company that produces egg cartons, has announced that from now on it will make its cartons from pulp rather than from materials that are known to be harmful to the ozone layer.

Not only is "buying green" a growing priority among consumers, but people are also showing increasing responsibility when it comes to the bags they use to carry home what they buy. More and more consumers are using their own cloth bags instead of the paper and plastic bags usually provided by stores. And when they do use plastic bags, many of them ask if the plastic is biodegradable.

The Bible tells us that "whatever you do in word or deed, do all in the name of the Lord Jesus" (Colossians 3:17). Certainly this applies to our consumer habits. A book entitled *The Green Consumer* by John Elkington, Julia Hailes, and Joel Makower, provides some brilliant guidelines on how buying can be more Christian so far as the environment is concerned.[4]

Be Faithful in Little Things

Being Christian requires that we think globally but act locally. The Bible always calls us to do the things we can do in the places where we live our everyday lives and to rest assured that God will take care of the larger picture. God requires that we be faithful in those things He has given us to do right where we are, and not to be overwhelmed by the immensity of the overall problem of the pollution and destruction of His creation. Do what can be done, and He will do the rest. That realism is stated so well by the apostle Paul as he tells us, "Therefore, as we have opportunity, let us do good to all, especially to those who are of the household of faith" (Galatians 6:10). I want to emphasize the words *Therefore, as we have opportunity.* God does not hold us responsible for what we *cannot* do, but He does hold us responsible for what we *can* do. And here are a handful of things each of us can do that will make a difference:

- You can plant a tree. If every American would plant a tree, more than a billion pounds of "greenhouse gases" would be removed from the atmosphere every year.

- Cut down on junk mail. Just cutting down on the junk mail that you alone get over the course of a year would save one and a half trees. Christians often get on the mailing list of far too many missionary societies. Make sure that you are on the mailing lists of only those missionary organizations that you are really interested in supporting with gifts or prayer. Write to Mail Preference Service,[5] and tell them to stop mailing you stuff. You'll save them money, and you'll save trees. Stewardship of time requires that you cut back on junk mail. Consider the fact that the average American spends eight full months of his or her life just opening and looking over junk mail!

- Use a clean detergent. Use a low-phosphate or phosphate-free detergent. Phosphates do make clothes cleaner but at a great cost to the environment. They fertilize algae to the point where it grows out of control. When the algae die, the bacteria that cause it to decompose use up vast amounts of oxygen needed by other plants and marine life. The result of all of this is that lakes and ponds across the nation are dying.

- Use latex paint. As much as 60 percent of all hazardous waste dumped by individuals comes from oil-based paint or paint products.

- Make sure that your tires are properly inflated (more than 50 percent of them are not). Underinflation can waste up to 5 percent of a car's fuel by increasing "rolling resistance." If all Americans made sure that their tires were inflated to the prescribed level, we would save up to two billion gallons of gasoline a year.

- Cut down on the use of batteries. Batteries contain heavy metals that contribute to hazardous wastes. The most common of these dangerous metals is mercury. Just to give you some idea about the effects of batteries, consider the hatmakers of the seventeenth century. They used mercury to treat felt. Since mercury is very toxic and quickly poisons the brain, many of the hatmakers were literally driven crazy, hence the expression "mad as a hatter." You can make the world a better place simply by using rechargeable batteries whenever possible. You'll save a lot of money too.

Pray for the Environment and All Its Creatures

Since I am listing practical things individuals can do to make being green a part of their everyday lives, it is only proper that I finalize the list by stating the most practical thing of all—*pray*. Prayer changes things! We should not only have special prayers on special occasions in which we hold environmental concerns before the Lord. I am suggesting that prayer for the environment be a part of our everyday personal devotions.

First of all, we should pray for forgiveness. What we have done to wreck God's creation is sinful, and we should repent. We should confess how our consumer life-styles have contributed to the pollution of the rivers, lakes, oceans, and the air we breathe. Having confessed, we should repent and ask the Lord to guide us into more careful living.

We should be praying for forgiveness for what we have done to animals. John Wesley was quite ready to acknowledge our sins against those poor creatures in the animal kingdom that have had to endure so much unnecessary suffering at our hands. Prayers heighten our consciousness of our sins and are a primary means that God uses to help us change our ways. The Holy Spirit will help us as we pray (Romans 8:26) and will guide us into ways in which we can show more of His love to creatures that are of great concern to Him.

Second, ask God to intervene in matters related to the environment that are in the news. Daily you can read in the newspapers about terrible things that are going on. For instance, following the Gulf War hundreds of oil wells were left burning, and the oily smoke and fumes that were exploding into the atmosphere for months afterward proved to be an ecological disaster. Asking God to stop the burning and restore the environment should have been in the prayers of Christians everywhere. Reports of environmental catastrophes like this one are part of everyday life. They include stories of oil spills, destruction of the ozone layer of the atmosphere, and destruction of the rain forests. All of these matters should be put daily before the Lord.

Last, we should be praying for the church, that God might awaken its people to their responsibility to care for His creation and be His agents for renewing what has been devastated by uncaring humanity.

What I find intriguing is that children find nothing strange about thanking God for nature and praying for His protection of the animals that are dear to them. The prayers of the little girl at her bedside thanking God for flowers and birds, and of the small boy at the table asking God to bless his puppy and to make his sick cat well again, these seem like natural prayers. What I am asking is simply that we all become like little children in order to be part of God's kingdom.

13

AND NOW
THE RED FLAGS

*Warnings to Keep Us Out
of the New Age Movement*

If we're serious about leading our society in a commitment to saving the environment, we will have to work with people outside the church and that means we will inevitably end up in dialogue with New Agers. They are everywhere. It is almost impossible these days to go to a conference dealing with ecological issues without meeting them. They wrote many of the books on the environment. And what they say and how they say it is often attractive enough to seduce the unprepared into a mind-set estranged from biblical Christianity. This has happened time and time again. Some of the most prominent thinkers in the New Age movement started off as rather traditional Christians, seeking ways of thinking about nature that might raise the church's consciousness on environmental issues and concerns.

The increasing affinity the New Age movement has with the environmental movement has made many evangelical leaders suspicious of anyone who is involved in creation-care concerns. They have seen too many cases in which involvement with environmental issues was the first step into the strange, cultic world of New Age thinking. They are aware that, in some extreme cases, environmental concerns have led church members into the occult and even into Satanism.

Obviously we cannot abandon a cause that is so central to the biblical message about the kingdom of God simply because it has been joined by some who are anti-Christian. Otherwise, off-the-wall religious groups could drive us out of almost any worthwhile enterprise or movement simply by joining it. We must get smart enough to figure out where, when, and how dangerous ideas creep into our worldview. That is why I need to present some warnings here and now. That is why I must run up some red flags.

WARNING 1: MAKE SURE YOUR SPIRITUAL EXERCISES AND WORSHIP ARE CHRISTIAN

Christians often want to be open-minded and accepting of religious ideas and practices which seem more attuned to the spiritual qualities of creation than those generally found in the church. This, unfortunately, can get them involved with strange things, as often demonstrated at the conclaves of many mainline denominations.

At one such gathering there were extensive readings from *Black Elk Speaks*, a book that carried us into the spiritual relationship Native Americans have with nature. What troubled me was that these readings were treated as though they possessed more truth than the Bible.

There have been meetings of the World Council of Churches and the National Council of Churches in which liturgies and meditations from various mystical religions have been the essence of the worship services. And while I am more than ready to admit that there is a great deal we can learn from other religions, I also believe that these practices can have a very seductive influence on the Christian community.

We ought to remember that in the world of ancient Israel, the Jews often flirted with and were seduced by the religion of the Canaanites. They found the worship of nature and the mystical relationships with the earth espoused by their Canaanite neighbors very attractive.

This pagan worship of nature led the Jews away from God and made them idolaters. I am afraid that in some respects, history is repeating itself. I see signs in certain quarters of contemporary Christianity, even as there were in ancient Israel, that people are looking to pagan religions for inspiration and guidance. Environmental concerns can easily pave the way for all of this. Without a biblically based theology of creation, Christians who want to understand nature in spiritual terms can all too easily find themselves involved with pagan religions.

Matthew Fox, the Roman Catholic priest and guru of many in the New Age movement, is a blatant example of how easy it is to cross the line from Christianity into paganism. His deep respect for the insights of Native

Americans led him to adopt some of their religious forms for experiencing religious ecstasy. He and a handful of others get into a dugout that is then heated with hot coals. The temperature is driven up to the boiling point, and those who are in the hot box nearly suffocate and perspire until they are delirious. Meanwhile they also supposedly enjoy mystical experiences. According to Matthew Fox, in the euphoria that accompanies this process, he receives spiritual truth and a sense of enlightenment about nature.[1]

Perhaps I should not judge what I have not experienced, but my view of what God has revealed in Scripture drives me to do just that. I have a deep sense that whatever God wants us to experience about Himself has been described in Scripture and, more specifically, in the life of Christ. I believe that in Him and in the scriptural message that provides the context and background is the fullness of God (Colossians 2:9). Anybody who tries to add to or subtract from this revelation and from the means for spiritual ecstasy prescribed by Him and His Word is making a serious mistake. And that goes for those practices and rituals prescribed by Matthew Fox.

The Roman Catholic church silenced Fox for a whole year. It forbade him, upon threat of excommunication, to promote his ideas about how to spiritually relate to nature. The Vatican did not want Fox teaching that the techniques used by Native Americans to achieve oneness with nature were Christian disciplines. And while I hesitate to support any tendency by ecclesiastical bodies to silence free expression of religion, I can understand Roman Catholic leaders contending that if Fox does continue his propagation of Native American religion, he ought to do it outside their church.

WARNING 2: THERE IS A VAST DIFFERENCE BETWEEN SENSING A UNITY WITH NATURE AND ADVOCATING UNION WITH NATURE

The call to *union* with nature which New Age gurus advocate is part of pagan religion and is also a major emphasis of Eastern religions. To sense ourselves as part of God's creation and to be able to recognize a certain unity with the rest of nature as we worship God is a good thing. But to treat nature as some kind of spiritual personality with whom we can merge through meditation and psychic surrender is a serious mistake. God breathed His own breath only into the human race. Only we are created in God's image.

Humans have a level of consciousness that makes them transcend the rest of nature. We must not treat nature as some kind of spiritual entity, as though we owe it homage and surrender. Any talk of yielding ourselves to the forces of nature so as to experience union with it is certainly outside Christian thinking.

Christianity is about getting to know and worship God as He has expressed Himself in Jesus Christ. The God who confronts us as a person is our salvation. To Him and to Him alone, we surrender.

As we come to Christ in praise and love, we can join with nature, which also was destined to worship Him. But even as we participate with nature in glorifying God, we do so in a way that is qualitatively different and superior. Just as God's ways are not our ways and His thoughts are not our thoughts (Isaiah 55:8), so our ways are not nature's ways, and our thoughts are infinitely different from any kind of thinking that goes on in the biosphere or ecosphere of creation.

Furthermore, salvation comes not when we yield to *Gaia* (the "in" term for Mother Earth among ecologists) or to some other designation which would make our physical world into some kind of deity; it only comes in knowing and yielding to the person of Jesus Christ. Union with a universe which is defined as a spiritual deity is far removed from the Christian belief that there is only one God, and that He is transcendent over all He created.

God uses nature, and through it He gives us messages which offer us inklings and hints of His power and majesty. But He uses nature like we use telephones, as an instrument through which He speaks to us. Just as we are separate from the telephones we speak through, so God is separate from the creation through which we sometimes receive messages from Him. Thinking that we should become unified with nature just because God sometimes whispers messages through it makes as much sense as some romantic lovingly giving himself to a plastic telephone simply because the sounds of his sweetheart are sometimes heard through the thing.

Some theologians, like Grace Jantzen in her book *God's World, God's Body*, suggest that we look at the world as the embodiment of God.[2] Jantzen invites us to look at the world as the body in which God dwells in much the same way as I look upon my own flesh as an embodiment for me. Her theology would have us view any harm that we do to creation to be harm against our God.

Such a theology would provide a strong imperative for creation-care, but that does not mean that it is true. The neo-orthodox theologian, Karl Barth, contended that God is "totally other" than His creation, and the biblical case that he makes for this point seems irrefutable. To contend that the world is God's body is too close to pantheism for comfort, and church councils long ago settled the question as to whether or not pantheism can be a legitimate Christian theology.

WARNING 3: WE MUST NOT THINK THAT ALL LIFE IS OF EQUAL VALUE

There are those who believe that animals are just as precious to God as people are and that the rights of animals are on a par with the rights of human beings. There are others who even go so far as to claim that flowers and trees have just as much a right to life and well-being as humans do. And they contend that the former ought not be sacrificed to sustain the lives of people. As a case in point, there was a student of mine who went far beyond being a vegetarian. This particular student confined his diet to seeds and nuts. He believed that willfully killing plants for food was sinful.

Evangelical Christianity rejects any such belief system. While we sense something sacred in all of life, because we claim that all life is sustained by God, we nevertheless hold to a belief in what Arthur Lovejoy has called "the great chain of being"; we believe that there is a hierarchy in God's creation.[3] At the top of the hierarchy is Jesus, whose name is above every other name and whose standing gives Him preeminence over all the rest of God's creatures both in heaven and on earth.

We perceive that this "great chain of being" is in the writings of the psalmist:

> When I consider Your heavens,
>   the work of Your fingers,
> The moon and the stars,

which You have ordained,
What is man that You are mindful of him,
And the son of man that You visit him?
For You have made him a little lower
    than the angels,
And You have crowned him
    with glory and honor.
You have made him to have dominion
    over the works of Your hands;
You have put all things under his feet,
All sheep and oxen—
Even the beasts of the field,
The birds of the air,
And the fish of the sea
That pass through the paths of the seas.
O LORD, our Lord,
How excellent is Your name in all the earth!

                              (Psalm 8:3–9)

This chain of being places us above the animals. And Jesus Himself declares that we are worth more than the animals.

We assume that the animals are more important in God's scheme of things than are the plants and the trees. In reality, we Christians believe that Genesis 1 tells us the order of things. Those creations of God that were the last to be spoken into existence are the most important, and those that were created first are the least important. The earth and the stars were first to be created so they are at the bottom of the chain of being. Vegetation is next in the creation plan, and thus there is a higher value placed on plants and trees than on earth and stars. Later come the fish and the birds and the other animals which, consequently, stand higher in God's hierarchy. And finally, God creates the human male and female, thus giving to humanity its primary status in the world of nature.

Any theology or mystical philosophy that levels that hierarchy is contrary to the will of God and should be regarded with more than passing questioning. Christian orthodoxy requires the hierarchy prescribed by Scripture. All life is not of equal value. Did not Jesus Himself say:

> Are not two sparrows sold for a copper coin? And not one of them falls to the ground apart from your Father's will. But the very hairs of your head are all numbered. Do not fear therefore; you are of more value than many sparrows. (Matthew 10:29–31)

In everyday life, this means that while unnecessary killing is deplorable, it is not sinful to sacrifice that which is lower on the creation hierarchy of life for that which is higher. To sacrifice animals to sustain human life is moral.

There are some Christians who have made being vegetarians a requisite for all other Christians, but there is no scriptural support for this. The Bible gives clear evidence that eating meat is permissible:

> So God blessed Noah and his sons, and said to them: "Be fruitful and multiply, and fill the earth. And the fear of you and the dread of you shall be on every beast of the earth, on every bird of the air, on all that move on the earth, and on all the fish of the sea. They are given into your hand. Every moving thing that lives shall be food for you. I have given you all things, even as the green herbs." (Genesis 9:1–3)

In the New Testament, God gives Peter a vision that reaffirms His approval of eating meat (Acts 10:10–15). Being a vegetarian does have benefits for a hurting planet with limited resources. Each vegetarian allows fifty-five acres of land to be turned into grain production that otherwise would be used for cattle grazing. But the Bible does not specifically condemn eating meat.

Personally, I think that the Seventh Day Adventists have the right idea. They strongly urge their people to refrain from eating red meat, primarily for health reasons. They point out that vegetarians are much less likely to have heart trouble and get cancer. But even with the Seventh Day Adventists, this is only a strong recommendation, not a command. Eating meat in and of itself is not a sin.

There is one more thing to consider. If you have a pet, why not make the pet into a vegetarian? One out of every five people in the United States owns a dog. Each year, Americans buy their one hundred million cats and dogs approximately five billion dollars worth of food. Consider the fact that most of these pet foods come from the same slaughterhouses that produce flesh intended for human consumption. Dogs and cats are not naturally vegetarians, but they can live on vegetarian diets quite well. There are all kinds of "vege-pet" supplements. Check them out at stores. There is a book entitled *Vegetarian Cats and Dogs* by James Peden that gives good recipes for animals.

WARNING 4: KNOW THAT GOD, NOT HUMANITY, CONTROLS THE FUTURE OF PLANET EARTH

One of the main emphases of the New Age movement is the role that it defines for the human race. Most of those who identify with this strange mixture of Eastern religion, the Human Potential movement, and the occult have this in common: They claim a godlike character for mere mortals and declare that we have the power to determine our own destiny.

New Agers commonly hold to a belief that if we can just escape from what they claim is our limited understanding of ourselves and affirm our true powers as divine beings, we can create a utopian future for ourselves. Of course, the down side of their beliefs is that if we fail to realize our potential and properly control our destiny, then destruction and eventual oblivion will be our lot.

It is easy to see how New Age teachings lead to a way of thinking that makes us, as human beings, completely responsible for what happens on earth. We become the masters of the world and the captains of our fate. In the New Age movement, humanism becomes a religion in which we are the gods who determine whether life or death will be the future not only for the human race but also for the rest of God's creation.

The future, I am happy to announce, has already been decided by God. The Scriptures tell us that all things are ultimately going to work together for good (Romans 8:28). Anyone reading the Bible who skips ahead to read how it all ends will know the good news—Jesus wins and the kingdoms of this world become the kingdom of our God! I have every confidence that the world will end by being transformed into all that God wants it to be. There will be a new heaven and a new earth (Revelation 21:1) brought in by the One who makes all things new.

What I believe the Bible teaches is that God has already begun to transform the world through His people in the church. That work includes bringing other people into a personal relationship with Christ wherein they acknowledge Him as Lord of their lives. It also includes the transformation of all the social structures of our society such as the family, government, business and professional organizations, the educational systems, and recreational life. I also believe that as God does His work through His people, He will act to save all of nature from destruction. The environment will be rescued and renewed. *He* will do it. He will work through His people, but it will be *His* work. We are not the ones who can save the planet. At best, we are instruments of the one and only God who is "from everlasting to everlasting."

As God works through His church, we should recognize that there is more to saving His creation than what He does through us. The church is His first and primary means of working to rescue the world from corruption and decay. But insofar as the church does not heed His call to be His rescuers of creation, He will use instruments outside the church to accomplish His will. I believe that because of the slow response of the church to environmental concerns, God is even now using groups like Greenpeace, the Audubon Society, the Sierra Club, and the National Wildlife Federation to carry out His renewal plan for our small planet. Furthermore, we have this warning in Romans 9 to 11 that if the church refuses to do His will and carry out His mission, then He will abandon the church as His prime instrument for salvation even as He once abandoned Israel for its refusal to carry out His mission in history. We in the church must be about the tasks God has given us to do lest the privilege of doing them be taken from us.

Saving planet earth is God's work. He is the author and finisher of our salvation and of the salvation of our planet (Hebrews 12:2). Any theology or philosophy that suggests that we alone determine the fate of the planet plays to our arrogant tendencies and leads us into sin.

We also must be aware of the fact that, as we attempt to live out our calling to participate in rescuing creation, we will encounter powerful opposition. Orchestrated by the Evil One, that opposition will be very effective. Satan is a very real enemy in our battle to save our environment. We are not struggling simply against a few misinformed citizens who can be turned around by attending a forum on environmental issues. We are, as the Scriptures say, fighting against principalities and powers in high places (Ephesians 6:12).

This means that in our own strength, we would lose in the struggle to save our planet from ecological disaster. But the good news is that He who is in us is greater than he who is in the world (1 John 4:4). We, therefore, can cry out with confidence to those who doubt what we can do, "If God is for us, who can be against us?" (Romans 8:31).

In the end, our limited efforts are not the whole story. That is why we Christians find so much hope in the second coming of Christ. We know that one day He who saved us by His blood will return to earth in triumph and will bind the forces that have been destroying our planet and will Himself bring all dead things back to life again in order to renew all of creation. The prophet Ezekiel envisioned this day when he declared:

> He said to me, "Son of man, have you seen this?" Then he brought me and returned me to the bank of the river. When I returned, there, along the bank of the river, were very many trees on one side and the other. Then he said to me: "This water flows toward the eastern region, goes down into the valley, and enters the sea. When it reaches the sea, its waters are healed.

And it shall be that every living thing that moves, wherever the rivers go, will live. There will be a very great multitude of fish, because these waters go there; for they will be healed, and everything will live wherever the river goes. It shall be that fishermen will stand by it from En Gedi to En Eglaim; they will be places for spreading their nets. Their fish will be of the same kinds as the fish of the Great Sea, exceedingly many. But its swamps and marshes will not be healed; they will be given over to salt. Along the bank of the river, on this side and that, will grow all kinds of trees used for food; their leaves will not wither, and their fruit will not fail. They will bear fruit every month, because their water flows from the sanctuary. Their fruit will be for food, and their leaves for medicine." (Ezekiel 47:6–12)

With a visionary hope like this, let us be about our Father's business. Let us work to clean up the environment, rescue the creatures of God that are threatened by human abuse, and become good stewards of the rich creation He has given to us to enjoy.

THE HEART OF THE MATTER

Environmentalism as the Fruit of the Spirit

Spirituality and creation-care are tied together. To be properly committed to the one should lead us inevitably to commitment to the other. If there is anything that becomes clear as you read the writings of those Christians who have stood historically as models of spiritual maturity, it is that along with their deepening awareness of God came a growing sensitivity to nature and a profound sorrow about its sufferings.

To know God is to care. More specifically, it is to care for all that concerns God. That means, of course, that first and foremost we will be concerned about God's people and their salvation. But getting into the heart of

God also will lead us into a profound sensitivity to animals. As we take on the mind of Christ (Philippians 2:5) through prayer and meditation, the desire to see His salvation extended to all of His creatures will become very much a part of our thinking. As we grow in Christ, we cannot help but become concerned about all the living things of the world. We will love them because He created them and because He sustains them by His grace (Colossians 1:17).

A genuine devotional life will lead the Christian into a special consciousness of creation, which is the best basis for environmental responsibility. Being spiritual, we will discover, leads increasingly to a demonstration of what the apostle Paul calls the "fruit of the Spirit." He writes:

> But the fruit of the Spirit is love, joy, peace, longsuffering, kindness, goodness, faithfulness, gentleness, self-control. Against such there is no law. (Galatians 5:22–23)

With the help of Andrew Basden's reflections in *The Industrial Christian Fellowship Pamphlet*, I would like to expound on that Scripture by reviewing each of these words that so carefully define the nature of true spirituality.

LOVE GOD'S CREATION

Love God's creation because God loves it and sent His Son to deliver it from corruption (John 3:16).

Love creation because God is holding it together by His grace. He is the One who is maintaining the unity of every atom and of every molecule, and as the giver of all life, He is the One who is sustaining every creature that walks, flies, or even crawls across the face of our fragile planet.

Love God's creation as His Son did during those limited days when His feet felt the texture of fertile soil, His hands petted the heads of sheep and cows, and His eyes focused intensely on the glories in nature from lilies to sunsets.

Love creation because it is a special gift of love from the One who knows each one of us by name and who calls each of us to be a part of His kingdom.

HAVE JOY IN HIS CREATION

Learn to laugh with the waters that spill over rocks and rush through rapids. Learn to sing with the birds in the morning, and learn to clap your hands with the rustling leaves of the trees. Learn how to have fun with puppies and thrill with the lightning bugs that fly around on hot summer nights.

Enjoy the taste of clean air as you climb some hills, and enjoy the taste of cool water as you quench the thirst that comes from hard work.

Feel the ecstasy of all the things that you can smell and touch and hear in this too-often-taken-for-granted world. Taste and see that the Lord is good (Psalm 34:8). And learn to be thrilled with the extraordinary ordinary things that are all around you.

When I think like this, I always recall the story of Fyodor Dostoyevski, who as a young man was once dragged before a firing squad for being a political subversive. Dostoyevski was blindfolded, ordered to make his confession, say his prayers, and then wait for the bullets to pierce his heart.

He heard the commands of the officer telling the soldiers to get ready. He heard the order given to fire. He even heard the guns go off. But he felt nothing.

The guns were loaded with blanks. The czar had brought the young revolutionary to the brink of death only to let Dostoyevski know in this emotionally devastating fashion that his life had been spared.

In retrospect, Dostoyevski considered what had happened to him that day one of the most blessed things that could happen to anyone. To go through the whole process of dying without really dying allowed him to appreciate, at a heightened level of awareness, life and all that God gives us in His creation.

The day that Dostoyevski was supposed to die, he had enjoyed the taste of food as never before. When they took him into the courtyard where he supposedly was going to be shot, he enjoyed the sensation of the sun beating and burning his skin and the feel of the wind blowing on his face. As he experienced what he was certain would be his last few moments of life, his senses were intensely receptive to the thousands of sounds and smells that were all around him. In those last few moments before the gunfire rang out that was supposed to end it all, he enjoyed God's world and soaked in all that he could of His creation.

The young man later recalled that he enjoyed more of God's creation on that day of his expected execution than he had in all of his life. Through it all, he gained the capacity to enjoy God's creation as few men or women in time and history have ever enjoyed it.[1]

This incredible enjoyment of God's creation described so well by Dostoyevski can belong to all of us, to anyone who surrenders to the Holy Spirit. It is one of the marks of being close to God. To grow in Christ is to learn to "die daily" and thus to learn to live joyfully in the midst of a world alive with wonder.

PURSUE PEACE WITH CREATION

End the warfare that has established us as conquerors who seek to dominate and exploit nature. Replace that warfare with the *shalom* of God where harmony and mutual well-being are the order of the day.

With the peace God gives comes an end to the violence that has raped the rain forests of the Amazon, slaughtered the great whales of the oceans, and torn up the green hillsides of the countryside with strip mines. If you follow in the steps of the Prince of Peace, you will walk among the animals in such a way that they will believe you are their friend. You will be able to eat the fruit of the trees in fields with constant appreciation for the provisions of God. And you will be able to breathe so deeply that your lungs will heave with the relaxed sighs that only belong to those who have learned to be at home in the world.

HAVE PATIENCE WITH THE NATURAL PROCESSES

Creation has its own timetable and rhythm, and we must learn to synchronize our lives with its ebbs and flows. All things in nature happen in the fullness of time, and those who are patient and learn to "go with the flow" will be relaxed even as the world rushes about in its stressed and frenzied manner.

Be like the farmer described by Jesus who knew that after the seeds had been planted nothing could be rushed:

> And He said, "The kingdom of God is as if a man should scatter seed on the ground, and should sleep by night and rise by day, and the seed should sprout and grow, he himself does not know how. For the earth yields crops by itself: first the blade, then the head, after that the full grain in the head. But when the grain ripens, immediately he puts in the sickle, because the harvest has come." (Mark 4:26–29)

Learn from nature that everything has to take its course and that when life is rushed, nothing is really gained. Nature refuses to keep pace with us, and those who want to live in tune with God's creation must learn to slow down and wait for things to happen as they should.

I talked with a father who was overwrought because his son was not walking in the ways of the Lord. The father was complaining because he had done all that he could to plant the seeds of faith in his boy and to nurture his son in the ways of the kingdom of God. Yet his son did not walk with God.

I asked the father to read the parable cited above and to be patient. In due season, I told him, referring to Galatians 6:9, he would reap if he just did not give up.

We must not only love creation, enjoy it, and live at peace with it, but we must allow creation to teach us its special lessons about time. From nature, we can glean that blessing called patience.

BE KIND AND GOOD TOWARD CREATION

The great philosopher Immanuel Kant stated in his *Lectures on Ethics,* "If man is not to stifle human feelings, he must practice kindness toward animals, for he who is cruel to animals becomes hard also in his dealings with men. We can judge the heart of man by his treatment of animals."

The actor James Mason refused to play in a film containing a cock-fight scene. He said, "I don't think you should hurt or kill animals just to entertain an audience. Animals should have some rights."[2]

Most of us know that the evangelical social reformer William Wilberforce was a primary force in England for the abolition of slavery and that he worked day and night to protect children by helping to pass child labor laws. But not many of us realize that this great Christian reformer also was a primary force behind the founding of the Royal Society of the Prevention of Cruelty to Animals. Not many know that the same Holy Spirit who gave Wilberforce a deep compassion for slaves and for children also gave him a bleeding heart for suffering animals.[3]

Wilberforce made kindness and goodness toward animals a crucial part of his spirituality, and if he were with us today, he would teach us to do the same.

The philosopher Immanuel Kant, the actor James Mason, and Christian reformer William Wilberforce had this in common: Each believed that humans should show goodness and kindness toward animals. But the Bible goes beyond them and teaches that goodness and kindness must be shown toward the rest of creation too. Chemicals that hurt the soil are not kind or good to the earth. Industrial waste dumped into the ocean reflects an indifference to nature that can only be considered sin. Those of us who pollute the air are living contrary to the will of God. The ways we live in this world should express the spiritual fruits of goodness and kindness.

Each one of the astronauts who had the privilege of walking on the moon and looking back at the earth has become an environmentalist. They all talked about how fragile and delicate our planet looked to them from "way out there." In space, each of them had the same awesome sense that the earth was somehow inviting them to care for it with lovingkindness and tender hearts.

LET US BE FAITHFUL IN OUR STEWARDSHIP OF CREATION

Creation is a trust from God. When Christ returns, He will ask what we have done with it. He will want to know if we watered it, nurtured it, and encouraged its fruitfulness, or if we abused it, forsook it, and ignored its needs.

God expects us to take what He has given us and do more than just return it to Him the way we received it. He expects us to care for His creation, to bless it, and to make it more fruitful. He expects us to be faithful servants who attend to His creation.

One day, God will call us before His judgment seat, and we can be certain that He will ask us to give an account of what we have done to the world which He has entrusted into our hands (Matthew 25:14-30).

A preacher once made a call on one of his neighbors, a farmer who, sad to say, had never had much time for the church.

The preacher found his neighbor out in his fields checking on the wheat growing there. Trying to get the farmer talking on religious things, the preacher said, "That's a fine field of wheat you and the Lord are growing together!"

There was no response from the farmer who acted as though the preacher wasn't even there. So the preacher let his well-chosen words fly a second time. "That's a fine field of wheat you and the Lord are growing together!"

Still there was no response. The old farmer acted as though he hadn't heard a thing.

But when the preacher made the same pronouncement a third time, the old farmer answered, "You should have seen this field last year when the Lord had it all to Himself."

Both the farmer and the preacher have truth to give us. The preacher was right to remind the farmer that all that he ever could hope to accomplish would be because of a partnership with God. The farmer might till the soil and plant the seed, but God makes the rain fall, the sun shine, and the wheat grow. On the other hand, the farmer was right to acknowledge that without the proper development, the land would not produce much and indeed would be little more than a field overgrown with weeds. Faithful stewardship requires that we take what God places in our hands, especially His creation, and care for it as a faithful service to Him.

BE GENTLE WITH CREATION

The Scriptures invite us to walk softly upon the earth. We should be meek and know our place in the natural order of things.

To be spiritual requires that we abandon the pushiness so characteristic of the powerful. The ways of Christ are not the ways of those who demand that their wants be gratified regardless of the cost and the suffering.

Gentleness and meekness are contrary to the ways of a world that worships those who wield power and who force their will on everyone and everything around them.

Once, when I was a boy sitting in church listening to a sermon on the Beatitudes, I had a harsh reminder of the world's attitude toward gentleness and meekness. The minister had just finished reading the fourth of the Beatitudes, "Blessed are the meek: for they shall inherit the earth," when the cynical college student sitting next to me muttered, "They had better inherit it. It's the only way they'll ever get it."

The ways of the flesh are not the ways of the Spirit. And we are called to live after the ways of the Spirit, which are full of meekness and gentleness.

Our arrogance has brought havoc to the planet. We have lived as though we are the only ones with rights. We have trampled all over this planet and have stepped on every and any creature that dares to stand in our way.

We have gunned down the bison on the American plains. We have made ash trays out of the hands and feet of the African mountain gorillas. We have fashioned trophies from the heads of creatures God loves.

Our lack of meekness led to our abuse of the creatures of the earth, leaving the land a mess.

But the meek are humble. They know their limits, and they come to the world with a servant's attitude.

When I was a boy, my mother always made me clean up the messes I made. If my room was cluttered, I had to "pick it up." She would stand over me to make sure that I put everything back where it belonged.

It took a lot of time for her to do this. As a matter of fact, it took her more time and effort to see that I did what I was supposed to do than it would have required for her to do the work by herself.

Mom made sure I did some of the dirty work every day, like scrubbing out the garbage can or cleaning the insides of the toilets. She wasn't trying to make life tough for me or to make things easy on herself. She just wanted to make sure I didn't grow up thinking I was exempt from cleaning up the messes I had made. She didn't want me to think that I was too important for the dirty work that is part of responsible living.

It is time we all learn what my mother tried to teach me and apply it to creation-care. When we mess up God's creation, we must learn to clean things up. Whether it is air, water, or land, meekness helps us recognize that we are not exempt from cleaning up our messes. And when it comes to oil spills and toxic wastes, we must see that each of us answers the call to make everything like new again.

PRACTICE TEMPERANCE, BETTER KNOWN AS SELF-CONTROL

We live in a time when people seem unable to regulate their own behavior. Most people cannot control their desires even when self-destruction is the result. Appetites for alcohol, tobacco, and cocaine have come to dominate their lives. Sexual drives seem out of control as people risk families and reputations to gratify their hungers.

Selfishness and greed have reached epidemic levels. People seek to get what they want when they want it. We have abandoned moral norms. No one expects us to show loving concern for others. The world is out of control, and all of creation is suffering from the consequences. It is this uncontrolled selfishness that has motivated the destructive behavioral patterns that have polluted and corrupted our natural habitat.

However, the forces that keep us from giving nature some time to recuperate are demonic. We are not simply up against some bad habits that we can overcome through an effective educational program. The problem is more serious than that. The problem is spiritual. We are not fighting against flesh and blood, as the Scripture so perfectly explains; we struggle against principalities and powers. We are up against rulers in high places (Ephesians 6:12).

Our disregard for other people and for the requisites of a balanced ecological system stems from an evil spirit that fosters our lack of self-control. Consequently, this flaw in our personality cannot be overcome by good intentions or even by sheer determination of the will.

The ruined world which begs for a chance at renewal comes from a sinful life-style that is not likely to be abandoned by those of us who have become accustomed to its comforts. Only the miracle wrought by our repentance and willingness to yield to the work of the Holy Spirit offers any real hope.

The character of people must change. And that can happen only as the result of His work in our lives.

Our values and our definitions of what constitutes "the good life" must radically change, and that can occur when God breaks through our cultural system and gives us a glimpse of His kingdom and of His righteousness.

People who are motivated only by profit must not determine the future of the world. Jesus has shown us another and better way.

Too often, when I read the books or listen to speeches of environmentalists who are not Christians, I recognize a basic shortcoming. Too frequently, they build their pleas for temperance and self-control on enlightened self-interest. Adopting a more environmentally responsible life-style, they point out, is the only reasonable thing to do if we know what is good for us. But much more than that is needed. We, ourselves, have to become completely different people. An enlightened plea won't work. If we are ever going to change the world, our basic consciousness must be transformed and our essential selves converted.

I believe that a repentant people who have yielded their lives to Christ will find the strength to exercise the kind of self-control that the world needs. In Him, we will be able to escape the bondage to the culturally prescribed consumeristic life-style that has brought us to the brink of environmental disaster. I believe that in Him, we will be able to reject the comforts which we wrongly believe are both necessary and desirable. I believe that in His power, we will be able to opt for a thoughtful, careful way of living which will make concern for others and a sensitivity to God's creation the basic motivations for all that we will and do.

Those who would save the environment must themselves be saved. Those who would see a new heaven and a new earth that is full of His beauty and glory must, themselves, be filled with His beauty and glory.

The environment has an awesome resilience if we just give it a chance.

I have been amazed at how quickly the Alaskan coastline has shown signs of coming back to life and cleaning itself up since the horrendous Exxon oil spill. I have been pleasantly surprised to learn that fish and other forms of life have moved back up our nation's rivers. There is heartening news that the ozone level can build up again if we just give it some time.

There is hope. There is a future. There is victory. Hear now the word of the Lord:

> For this corruptible has put on incorruption, and this mortal has put on immortality. So when this corruptible has put on incorruption, and this mortal has put on immortality, then shall be brought to pass the saying that is written: "Death is swallowed up in victory."
>
> "O Death, where is your sting.
> O Hades, where is your victory?"
>
> The sting of death is sin, and the strength of sin is the law. But thanks be to God, who gives us the victory through our Lord Jesus Christ. Therefore, my beloved brethren, be steadfast, immovable, always abounding in the work of the Lord, knowing that your labor is not in vain in the Lord. (1 Corinthians 15:53–58)

NOTES

Chapter 1: Getting into It

1. Richard S. Greene, "Issues of the Wallet, Issues of the Heart," *The Earth Is the Lord's*, edited by Vicki Haterman (Altamonte Springs, FL: Accord Publishing House, 1990), 63.
2. Ibid.

Chapter 3: Beating a Bum Rap

1. Lynn White, Jr., "The Historical Roots of Our Ecological Crisis," *Science*, 10 March 1967, 1203–1207.
2. John Calvin, *Commentaries on the First Book of Moses Called Genesis*, Vol. 1, edited by John King (Edinburgh: Calvin Translation Society, 1847), 91–100.
3. *Animals and Christianity*, edited by Andrew Linzey and Tom Regan (New York: Crossroads Press, 1988), ix.
4. Joseph Sheldon, *Rediscovery of Creation* (Metuchen, NJ: The Scarecrow Press, Inc., 1992).

Chapter 4: What in the World Is God Doing?

1. Excerpted from *Have You Heard of the Four Spiritual Laws?* by Dr. Bill Bright, Campus Crusade for Christ, published by Here's Life Publishers, 1965. Used by permission.

Chapter 5: What the Thinkers Are Thinking

1. Martin Buber, *I and Thou* (New York: Scribner's, 1937).
2. John Wesley, *Sermons on Several Occasions*, Vol. 2, (London: Wesleyan Conference Office, 1874), 281–286.
3. Ibid.
4. Ibid.
5. C. S. Lewis, *The Problem of Pain* (London: Collins/Fontana Books, 8th edition, 1967), 125–128.
6. Ibid.

Chapter 6: God in the Chicken Coop

1. Patrick Goldring, *The Broiler House Society* (Leslie Frewin, 1969), 22.
2. John Hick, *Evil and the God of Love*, Fontana Library of Theology and Philosophy (London: Collins/Fontana Books, 4th edition, 1975), 345–353.
3. Pampllet printed by People for the Ethical Treatment of Animals.
4. Ibid.
5. Ibid.

Chapter 7: Paradise Lost

1. See Pierre Teilhard de Chardin, *The Phenomenon of Man* (New York: HarperCollins, 1975).
2. J. Milton Keynes, *General Theory of Employment, Interest, and Money* (New York: McGraw-Hill, 1953).
3. See Vernon Spraxton, *Teilhard de Chardin* (London: SCM Press, 1971).

Chapter 9: Missions with the World in Mind

1. Should you want to contribute to the work of Floresta, send your gifts to:
     Floresta
     1015 Chestnut Avenue
     Suite F2
     Carlsbad, CA 92008
2. Should you want more information and/or want to contribute to the support of Opportunities International, contact:
     Opportunities International
     P.O. Box 3695
     Oakbrook, IL 60522
3. E. F. Schumacher, *Small Is Beautiful* (London: Sphere, 1973).

4. Should you want more information and an application for the graduate program at Eastern College, write to:
> Office of Graduate Admissions
> Eastern College
> St. Davids, PA 19087

Chapter 10: Some New Wine in Old Wineskins

1. William M. Ruyan and T. O. Chisholm, "Great Is Thy Faithfulness." Copyright © 1923. Renewnal 1951 by Hope Publishing Company. All rights reserved. Used by permission.

Chapter 11: The Greening of the Church

1. The address of the Evangelical Association for the Promotion of Education is:
> E.A.P.E.
> Box 7238
> St. Davids, PA 19087–7238
2. For more information write to:
> World Vision
> 919 West Huntington
> Monrovia, CA 91016

and to:
> Compassion International
> 3955 Cragwood
> Box 7000
> Colorado Springs, CO 80933
3. See Linda Kanamine, "Budget Crises Fell Urban Area Tree Programs," *USA Today*, 13 November 1991, 10A.
4. Tim Cooper, *Green Christianity* (London: Hodder & Stoughton, 1990), 252–257.
5. For excellent guidance on church investments:
> The Interfaith Center on Corporate Responsibility
> 475 Riverside Drive
> Room 566
> New York, NY 10027

Chapter 12: Changing the World with a Majority of One

1. *The Animal Voice*, a magazine published by People for the Ethical Treatment of Animals.

2. John Elkington, Julia Hailes, and Joel Makower, *The Green Consumer* (New York: Penguin Books, 1991), 6ff.
3. Ibid.
4. Ibid.
5. To stop your name from being sold to most large mailing list companies, write to:

   Mail Preference Service
   Direct Mailing Association
   11 West 42nd Street
   P.O. Box 3861
   New York, NY 10163–3861

Chapter 13: And Now the Red Flags

1. Matthew Fox, *Original Blessing* (Santa Fe: Bear & Co., 1983).
2. Grace Jantzen, *God's World, God's Body* (Philadelphia: Westminster Press, 1984).
3. Arthur O. Lovejoy, *The Great Chain of Being* (Cambridge, MA: Harvard University Press, 1942).

Chapter 14: The Heart of the Matter

1. See Introduction (by Ernest J. Simmons) to Fyodor Dostoyevski, *Crime and Punishment* (New York: Random House, 1950), vii–viii.
2. Pamphlet printed by People for the Ethical Treatment of Animals.
3. Ibid.

SUBJECT INDEX

SCRIPTURE INDEX

ABOUT THE AUTHOR

*T*ony Campolo is a sociology professor at Eastern College in St. Davids, Pennsylvania, and the director of the Evangelical Association for the Promotion of Education. He is the best-selling author of numerous books, including: *20 Hot Potatoes Christians Are Afraid to Touch*, *Who Switched the Price Tags?*, *Wake Up America!*, *Partly Right*, *The Kingdom of God Is a Party*, and *It's Friday but Sunday's Comin'*.

Tony received his Bachelor's degree in sociology from Eastern College, his Master of Divinity and Master of Theology degrees from Eastern Baptist Theological Seminary, and his Ph.D. in sociology from Temple University. He lives in St. Davids with his wife, Peggy. They have two grown children and one grandchild.